Mike Carpenter

LAS VEGAS
THE GRAND

The Strip, the Casinos, the Mob, the Stars

CONTENTS

INTRODUCTION

Las Vegas is a very special city, perhaps unique in the world. For starters, it lies literally in the middle of nowhere. When it was born, there was no other human settlement within dozens of miles in every direction. It is also the only city in the world I know of to have been built for a sole, exclusive purpose: to entertain people. Which, even today, is its main reason for being, although over the years it has gained considerable importance in the US military (with the large Nellis Air Force Base nearby) and now hosts a university that's quite respected, as well as a number of companies, active especially in online commerce and logistics.

The birth of this city is very recent, to be placed in 1902 (as we shall see), but its growth was literally explosive. In the years of the great boom, from the early 90s of last century to the devastating recession started in 2007/2008, the telephone company was forced to print two telephone directories per year instead of the traditional annual directory all other cities are used to, in order to be able to stay ahead of the incredible speed at which the population of the area increased. Immigration from other parts of the United States to Las Vegas, sure enough, was akin to a flood. This was due to the seemingly inexhaustible employment opportunities offered by the hospitality industry, which includes hotels, casinos (which have always been the city's main attraction), restaurants and connected services, with far better wages than those offered in the rest of the country – as a result of tourists' generous tips –, and to the warm and dry climate, which many find extremely enjoyable.

One can surely say that, if its duration is very short, the intensity of this city's history is equally out of the ordinary. Moreover, this is a story that can be entirely told following the evolution of its casino hotels (resorts, as they are called today), because they have always been the ones to mark the city's rhythm, breath, succession of happy times and dark moments. In this book, I will concentrate only on the resorts risen along one of the most popular and celebrated boulevards in the world, the famous Las Vegas Strip (whose real name is Las Vegas Boulevard South). It is a road stretch of about four miles located south of the city of Las Vegas proper, which is now called Downtown Las Vegas. Technically, the Strip is not even part of the Las Vegas municipality, because it belongs administratively to Clark County.

So, it's the story of those four miles of road I'll recount. The reason is simple: for the tourist visiting Las Vegas today, this is by far the most important area, as it is unlikely someone from out of town will spend a great deal of time in the downtown area, visited mostly by locals.

No reason to be skeptical: what at first glance may look like an arid undertaking with no real causes for interest will soon show to be a veritable treasure trove of incredible adventures, extravagant and brave characters, grand dreamers and countless anecdotes. Get ready for a ride full of surprises through a century of unparalleled history. Welcome to fabulous Las Vegas!

1

THE BEGINNINGS, THE RAILROAD, THE DAM

The history of the area known as Las Vegas begins in 1829. At that time, what is now Nevada was part of Mexico. In fact, only in 1848, following the Mexican-American war, did Nevada pass under Washington's government, becoming the 36th State of the Union in 1864.

Let's go back to 1829: an expedition of Spanish explorers, headed by Antonio Armijo, runs through the valley that today goes under the name of Las Vegas Valley, when it comes to a series of water springs – today called Las Vegas Springs or Big Springs – that give rise to a kind of oasis. Hence the name "las vegas", which in Spanish means "the meadows". It is likely that no white man had set foot in the valley before then.

As is easily understandable, the presence of water in the middle of a dry area like that makes all the difference. It is believed that at that time the nearest water sources were on a horseback day from Las Vegas. We can safely say that, without the discovery of water in 1829, a significant human settlement would never have developed in this semi-desert area.

Fast forward until 1902, when a Montana senator named William Andrews Clark decides to connect the city of Los Angeles on the Pacific Coast to Salt Lake City, Utah, through a railroad line. Mister Clark was a great personality: a true tycoon of the mining industry, banker and – of course – active in the railroad industry (which, at the time, was experiencing its greatest expansion), Clark is considered one of the five hundred wealthiest Americans ever.

The route of this railway line was designed to go through the Las Vegas Valley and, to facilitate and speed up the construction work, it was decided to build a town from scratch in order to provide workers involved in the construction of the railway with a place to rest. As one can easily imagine, the aforementioned workers did not just rest in the newly-born "city" of Las Vegas. Let's say they thought it was okay to add a couple of more engaging activities: gambling and paid sex, both of which soon became a formidable economic development engine for a place born as an agglomeration of unadorned shacks and dormitories. Most of the railway company's employees arrived with their pockets full of cash and left broke. The foundation for the colossal expansion of one of the most celebrated cities – for better or worse – of our time had been laid.

Las Vegas was officially established in 1905 and became a municipality in 1911. As already mentioned, the main tourist area (the Strip) is not strictly part of Las Vegas, but of the unincorporated town of Paradise and is directly administered by Clark County, which is named – as you might guess – after William Clark. It should also be noted that in 1910 the State of Nevada decided to ban gambling, while in 1919 Prohibition laws made production, trade and consumption of alcohol throughout the country illegal. In this regard, the early 30s of the twentieth century represent a complete reversal: in 1931 gambling was legalized again in Nevada, while Prohibition was abolished in 1933.

And with that, the first brick for the construction of Sin City had been placed. But a vital element was still missing, considering we are in the middle of a very dry area: water and electricity capable of feeding the expansion of a place like this beyond the size of a small village. Thus, in the spring of 1931, construction work was started on one of the largest engineering projects in North America ever: the Hoover Dam. Or, more precisely, the Boulder Dam, which was named after the President of the United States who had decided to build it, Herbert Hoover (president from March 1929 to March 1933), only later by the new commander in chief, Franklin Delano Roosevelt (president from March 1933 to April 1945). In classic American style, to accommodate the thousands of workers involved in the construction of the dam a new town – Boulder City – was built from scratch, about twenty-five miles south-east of Las Vegas.

The triple purpose of the dam located on the Colorado River – in addition to providing thousands of jobs in the middle of the Great Depression – was to prevent periodic flooding, provide abundant irrigation water for crops and produce large amounts of electricity, to be split between Arizona, California and Nevada. The dam, costing $ 50,000,000 at the time (about $ 900 million 2017) and 122 casualties among workers (many deaths were simply caused by extreme climatic conditions), was delivered by the consortium of builders to the federal government on March 1, 1936. Two years ahead of schedule.

Everything is in place now. Mafia "families" of the East Coast are about to put their eyes (and hands) on this city surrounded by the desert. The birth of the myth is near.

2

ANTHROPOLOGICAL NOTES ON GAMBLING

If prostitution is – more or less jokingly – considered "the oldest profession in the world", we can safely argue that gambling is the oldest pastime in the world. Archaeologists have been able to find artifacts and other proof related to gambling in every ancient civilization we are aware of, with very few exceptions.

We know the Sumerians in Mesopotamia did play dice – perhaps as early as six thousand years ago – using *astragali* (talus bones) and later the Ancient Egyptians as well. Talus bones come from terrestrial animals, precisely from the area where the paw joins the ankle. They are also present in humans, located between foot and ankle. Being vaguely cubic in shape, they represent the oldest dice ever to be found. The Romans, much later, did invent – for the Western part of the world – the six-faced regular dice in use today, making them in the most diverse materials (ivory, wood, stone and amber). Dice similar to those used in Ancient Rome can be traced back to China since 2000 BC.

It is believed that, initially, the above mentioned dice were used for divination practices. Essentially, the purpose was to predict the future based on the outcome of a throw of *astragali*, each face having a different numerical value (just like today). From here to try to guess in advance what the outcome of the throw of the dice would be – perhaps adding a little bet to increase the suspense – nothing more than a very short step was needed.

This is to say that Las Vegas's success as a "city of sins", though having a very short history behind it, is deeply rooted in human habits as ancient as civilization itself (prostitution and gambling), that – incidentally – are in no way specifically American. The typical American aspect is – if anything – that of grandeur: to build an entire Mecca of games and fun somewhere in the desert and make it a tourist destination for forty million visitors a year.

3

THE GODFATHERS

In this chapter, I will briefly review the role played by organized crime in the development and control of numerous Las Vegas casinos. I will not focus on the downtown area, as the purpose of this work is mainly to illustrate the events shaping that part of the city which every contemporary visitor gets to know in 90% of the cases: the Strip. Downtown has been inexorably left behind by history, and it will never recover, for obvious reasons of lack of space: only along the Strip it is possible to build a mega-resort and only casino hotels of this type and size have proven to be really profitable.

With regard to organized crime, a short summary will do. I shall only delve into the details of Flamingo's history in a subsequent chapter, because it is well-documented and because it has been narrated in a way that's as spectacular as it is rich of inaccuracies in the 1991 film *Bugsy*, directed by Barry Levinson and with Warren Beatty as gangster Bugsy Siegel.

This aspect of Las Vegas's history is not the main topic of our book, especially since the grip of organized crime on the city has now largely waned – for reasons that shall be explained later – and therefore no longer represents a reality which a visitor will come in contact with in 2018. Also, it should be considered that *mafiosi* notoriously do not like to advertise their activities. This means that chronicles about this sector of the economy are often based on unreliable or at the very least inaccurate accounts.

From my point of view, the history of the Las Vegas Strip is articulated in three distinct periods, each with different features that are easily identifiable.

The first period goes from the 1940s to 1966. This period is characterized by the supremacy of organized crime mostly coming from the eastern coast of the United States (especially of Jewish and Italian origin) on the city. The second period runs from 1966 to 1989, from the inauguration of Caesars Palace by Jay Sarno to the birth of the Mirage by the hands of Steve Wynn. We can consider the Caesars Palace to be the progenitor of theme resorts, the first example of "entertainment architecture" in Las Vegas. Given the subsequent developments of the Strip, it is really impossible to overstate the importance of this step. Even the most luxurious hotels dotting the Strip at the time (Dunes, Sands, Desert Inn) simply could not compete with a jewel like the Caesars Palace. But this will be the topic of one of our next chapters.

I set the beginning of the third Strip development period at the inauguration of Steve Wynn's Mirage in 1989. The impact this resort and its creator had on the future of Las Vegas has no equal in the history of the city, in a way I shall examine in detail. Perhaps only Howard Hughes, for different reasons, can be considered equally important in allowing the Strip to become what it is now. We will also get to know Hughes in due course. We could argue that Las Vegas is currently in the fourth phase of its history, following the burst of the giant real estate bubble that occurred in 2007 and the fact that gambling giants now make most of their profits on the Asian market, thanks to their Macao operations.

But let's come to the core of this chapter. As we all know – thanks in no small part to a clever marketing campaign of Las Vegas's authorities – in the not so distant past almost all casinos were in the hands of the organized crime. The reasons for such a successful marriage are easy to understand. Firstly, at that time it was unlikely that a honest entrepreneur used to run a perfectly legitimate business would decide to invest his own money and energy in an activity that was considered dirty and sinful (keep in mind that we are talking about the years from World War II to the end of the 1960s). Gambling was one of those pastimes practiced by many but despised by everyone, at least in public (just like paid sex). Add to this that huge amounts of cash are exchanged every day in every casino and in every strip club, which provides two main benefits to organizations devoted to criminal activities: the ability to practice money laundering on a grand scale and the chance to easily make disappear large sums of money from the back exit, obviously tax-exempt.

In order to put an end to those illegal practices, a 1970 law, called the Bank Secrecy Act (BSA), was of fundamental importance. According to this law, every financial institution – including casinos – is required to report all cash transactions of $ 10,000 or more to the relevant government agencies. In presence of activities deemed suspicious, the obligation to report is triggered for any amount, even much smaller than the ten thousand dollars mentioned. In this case, it's called Suspicious Activity Report (SAR). It is quite obvious that, taken together, these two measures effectively eradicate any money laundering activity and greatly reduce the appeal of the casino industry for the organized crime. From time to time, the Internal Revenue Service (IRS) still finds, thanks to the law described above, US tax evaders who attend casinos with bankrolls higher than those they could afford based on their tax return.

Following properties on the Las Vegas Strip were under the direct or indirect control of various Mafia families in the 1950s and 1960s:
- Flamingo, inaugurated on December 26, 1946, to whose interesting story I will dedicate a comprehensive chapter;
- Desert Inn, inaugurated on April 24, 1950, controlled by Moe Dalitz, an associate of Meyer Lansky (real

name Meyer Suchowljansky, who also controlled the Flamingo);

- Sands, inaugurated on December 15, 1952, controlled by Salvatore 'Momo' Giancana (of clear Italian origin);
- Riviera, inaugurated on April 20, 1955, controlled by Anthony 'Big Tuna' Accardo (another *compare*);
- Dunes, inaugurated on May 23, 1955, controlled by Morris Shenker, a *Cosa Nostra* lawyer;
- Tropicana, inaugurated on April 3, 1957, controlled by Johnny Rosselli and Joe Agosto (real name Vincenzo Pianetti) on behalf of Frank Costello (real name Francesco Castiglia);
- Stardust, inaugurated on July 2, 1958, conceived by Tony 'The Hat' Cornero (who would die in 1955) and controlled by Accardo on behalf of the Mafia of Chicago;
- Aladdin, inaugurated on March 31, 1966, controlled by Sorkis Webbe, another Mob lawyer.

As you can see, it's no exaggeration to say that organized crime had put its hands on all of the most celebrated and best-known Strip properties. Until the late 1950s, godfathers could rule virtually undisturbed in Las Vegas, looking after their own interests without too much interference from the authorities. Exemplary cheat punishments (such as mangled hands in some utility room) and disappearances in the desert of unruly colleagues were common practice. It was only since the early 1960s that John Edgar Hoover's FBI, with the decisive support of then Attorney General

Robert Kennedy, started to face and solve once and for all the problem. It would become a twenty-year fight, eventually won in part thanks to techniques already employed against a famous gangster of the recent past: Al Capone. The federals, that is, chose to use the shortcut of tax evasion and administrative irregularities to force Mob bosses to sell – more or less voluntarily – their stake in Las Vegas casino hotels to less controversial entrepreneurs, rather than pursuing unlikely convictions for more serious offenses, in a field where a code of silence reigns supreme. These methods did prove to be winning, in no small part thanks to Howard Hughes, whose decisive role will be discussed later.

The last vestiges of the presence of the Mob in "fabulous" Las Vegas have been told with a certain adherence to the truth by Martin Scorsese in his magnificent movie *Casino*, of 1995. To this film – since it is directly linked to the present chapter – and to the unforgettable Rat Pack of Frank Sinatra I'll now dedicate two short chapters.

4

CASINO

In his masterpiece – one of many – of 1995, director Martin Scorsese describes the story contained in the book titled, you guessed it, *Casino*, a novel inspired by a true story (as we shall see), written by Nicholas Pileggi. Pileggi, previously author of *Wiseguy*, from which Scorsese drew inspiration for the movie *Goodfellas* in 1990, did collaborate with Scorsese on the screenplay of the film. The book and the film feature a certain Sam 'Ace' Rothstein (in Robert De Niro's memorable interpretation), whose character is based on the real Frank 'Lefty' Rosenthal, who worked in Las Vegas in the 1970s on behalf of Chicago's most powerful criminal organization, called "Chicago Outfit" or "Chicago Syndicate". Among the prominent figures of this Mafia "family" we find, over the decades, criminals like Giacomo 'Big Jim' Colosimo, Alphonse 'Al' Capone, Tony 'Big Tuna' Accardo, Salvatore 'Momo' Giancana, and many more.

Pileggi got the idea for his story in 1980, when he read in the *Las Vegas Sun* of an uproarious family clash between Rosenthal and his wife Geri McGee (Sharon Stone/Ginger McKenna in the film), a scene present toward the end of *Casino*. In order to simplify the story, De Niro/Rothstein only manages the Tangiers (a fictitious name), while in real life Rosenthal did manage the Stardust, Fremont, Marina and Hacienda casinos on behalf of his Chicago bosses. In fact, the story is set at the Stardust, though the interior sets have all been filmed at the Riviera, always between one and four at night, to minimize the disruption to normal casino routines. The exterior sets were all shot in Las Vegas, at various locations. The third protagonist of the story is Nicholas 'Nicky' Santoro, in the overwhelming performance of a great Joe Pesci, based on the figure of Tony 'The Ant' Spilotro, a gangster known for his brusque methods – often based on the use of uncontrolled brutality – as shown in the film.

Spilotro, who had five brothers – four of whom were involved in criminal activities like him –, would end up massacred by order of the Mob bosses he worked for, who were unsatisfied with his way of doing business in Las Vegas and elsewhere. His brother Michael was killed with him. Contrary to what is shown in the film, it seems that the two were murdered in a house in Bensenville, Illinois, on June 14, 1986, and only later buried in a hole in a wheat field at Enos, Indiana, where they were found nine days later.

Some trivia I came across during my research on this movie:

Apparently, Scorsese had considered a long list of

actresses for the role of Ginger McKenna, including Nicole Kidman, Cameron Diaz, Jodi Foster, Michelle Pfeiffer (who was launched when very young by Brian De Palma in *Scarface*), Jamie Lee Curtis, Madonna, Melanie Griffith, choosing Sharon Stone in the end. A very smart choice, considering that Stone did earn an Oscar nomination for this movie.

The scenes outside the fictional Tangiers were actually filmed outside the Landmark Hotel (inaugurated in 1969, closed in 1990 and imploded in November 1995), in front of the Las Vegas Hilton.

Do you remember the character of the Japanese high roller in the movie – Mr. Ichikawa – who, after winning big at the casino, is lured back with a trick and then loses millions? Well, it is a character inspired by a famous Japanese player named Akio Kashiwagi, who in the 1970s and 1980s was one of the "whales" – as the players who gamble at the highest limits are called – in Las Vegas. Unfortunately for him, part of his finances – exhausted by the end of the 1980s due to his losses at the casino tables – came from the Japanese Mafia, the hardly accommodating Yakuza, which apparently did not appreciate at all. As a logical consequence, Kashiwagi was assassinated in Tokyo in 1992, killed by a hit man with a samurai sword. Real life like out of a movie!

Scorsese was not allowed to mention the Stardust casino, so he just let play short pieces of the popular song *Stardust* (composed in 1927) thrice during the film as a sophisticated reference to the actual setting of the story.

You do remember – I guess – the short cameo by Oscar Goodman, not yet Las Vegas mayor, acting as De Niro/Rothstein's lawyer. In real life, Goodman had been the lawyer not only of Rosenthal, but also of Spilotro, Meyer Lansky and many other members of the Mob. Only in fabulous Las Vegas!

The scene, definitely for stronger stomachs, of the guy with his head squashed in a vise by Pesci/Santoro was inserted by Martin Scorsese on purpose, with the certainty that it would be cut off by the Motion Picture Association of America because of its extremely gory content. Scorsese hoped to obtain – through this cut – the green light for the other, numerous scenes of violence contained in the film. Contrary to his prediction, the MPAA had nothing to argue and the scene survived in the final cut.

5

OCEAN'S 11 AND THE RAT PACK

Talking about movies, let me tell you about Frank Sinatra and his Rat Pack.

In 1960 Frank and his friends, Dean Martin (real name Dino Paul Crocetti, of Italian origin), Sammy Davis Jr. (one of the first successful black entertainers), Peter Lawford (real name Peter Sydney Ernest Aylen, brother-in-law of president John F. Kennedy) and Joey Bishop (real name Joseph Abraham Gottlieb), descended upon Las Vegas for the shooting of *Ocean's 11*, directed by Lewis Milestone. I guess everybody knows the plot of the film from the remake of 2001, in which George Clooney took over Frank Sinatra's role as Danny Ocean, the boss of a gang of skillful robbers who want to clean out a number of Las Vegas casinos.

Within a few weeks, Frank, Dino and company made the Sands "the place to be". In fact, the movie was filmed there, and Sands' Copa Room saw the five friends perform each night at the end of the shooting, singing and entertaining the audience. The nights then went on at the tables. Thus, the Sands and the Copa Room became a legend forever.

Subsequently, both Frank Sinatra and the other

protagonists of *Ocean's 11* still performed at the Sands from time to time, singly or all together. Until the day when the management of the casino – recently taken over by Howard Hughes (it's 1967) – decided to cut Sinatra's credit line. He quickly packed up and chose to move a little further down the road, to the Caesars Palace. Not before being involved in a fist fight with casino manager Carl Cohen, of course.

The Sands – inaugurated on December 15, 1952 – was imploded in November 1996 to make room for the Venetian, not before being hit by a plane carrying a load of inmates that landed right in the lobby of the hotel, for the movie *Con Air* (released in 1997).

6

THE BOMB

Before delving into the most recent part of Las Vegas's fabled history, I could not abstain from devoting a brief chapter to one aspect of the city's history that's probably little known: the atomic bomb. To be precise, for a period of twelve years – from 1951 to 1963 – the US government had one thermonuclear bomb detonated every three weeks on average (that's over 200 in total) in an area called Nevada Test Site, just over 60 miles from Downtown Las Vegas. And we are talking about bombs far more powerful than those dropped on Japan during World War II.

Keep in mind that we were in the middle of the Cold War and the United States was seriously preparing for a possible armed conflict against the Soviet Union. Many Americans built anti-atomic shelters in their basements. The "funny" aspect of this story, if I may, is that Las Vegas residents – far from being upset – thought it best to take full advantage of this opportunity for tourist purposes too! The Las Vegas Visitors Authority went as far as to print a test calendar for visitors, which included a list of the best observation points in town to watch the explosions. By the way, it seems that a Desert Inn lounge, The Sky

Room, was a coveted place for tourists interested in witnessing this particular form of event, having a great panoramic view of the horizon in the direction of the detonation site.

It seems almost unnecessary to add that Sin City's enterprising merchants quickly launched "atomic cocktails" and even the Miss Atomic Bomb contest. Postcards, toys, sweets etc. were decorated with the mushroom cloud. Try to imagine what tourist appeal a place that advertises itself to be only 60 miles away from an area of atomic surface testing would have today. Clearly, at that time the health risks of such tests were not entirely understood...

In short, a lack of spirit of enterprise and of business acumen is not among Las Vegas residents' flaws!

7

THE PRECURSORS

Starting with this chapter, I will present all casino hotels built along the Strip, beginning with the first ever (while downtown, of course, casinos had existed long before that). For each one, the inauguration date and the closing date – where appropriate – will be indicated. In some cases I will add a more comprehensive description. The great Las Vegas characters who made the city the way it is today, however, shall be described extensively as soon as we reach the 1960s.

EL RANCHO VEGAS (1941 – 1960)
The El Rancho Vegas was the first casino with annexed hotel to open on the Strip (just below Sahara Av.), on April 3, 1941, by Thomas E. Hull. The cost of this casino hotel was $ 425,000 at the time (equivalent to $ 7.1 million today) and the hotel had, initially, 63 rooms. An additional 47 rooms were added later. It was here that the unforgettable Paul Newman married the beautiful Joanne Woodward on January 28, 1958. The two stayed together until the death of the great actor (September 26, 2008). A tale from a different time, if you will.

THE LAST FRONTIER (1942 – 2007)

The second casino hotel to rise along the Strip was the Last Frontier, inaugurated on October 30, 1942, later renamed New Frontier in April 1955. Here Elvis Presley made his Las Vegas debut in 1956, the city where he built his own immortal myth with 58 sold outs in the showroom of Kirk Kerkorian's International Hotel (now Westgate Las Vegas Resort & Casino, after many years as the Las Vegas Hilton). The Hungarian Gabor sisters (Zsa Zsa, Eva and Magda) did perform here in 1953 and, hear ye hear ye, the future US president Ronald Reagan once had a one-man-show in the same showroom, getting paid $ 30,000 ($ 275,000 today) for two weeks of performances in 1954. The property, built on the ashes of the Pair-O-Dice Club nightclub (later 91 Club, named after Highway 91, i.e. Las Vegas Boulevard), was eventually imploded in November 2007 to make room for the mega-resort project of 6,700 total rooms called The Plaza Las Vegas, which was nipped in the bud before the foundation stone could be laid by the Great Recession that started in 2007. Today it would be on the opposite side of the Strip from Steve Wynn's Encore.

GOLDEN NUGGET (1946 – still open)

As stated before, I am not going to examine the history of casinos located in the downtown area of the city (the actual Las Vegas), both because I am not really knowledgeable about it and because the history of Strip properties is far more relevant to a contemporary visitor. I'll make an exception for the Golden Nugget, which – in addition to being the most prestigious downtown property – marks the start of Steve Wynn's stunning career in the city (he owned the Golden Nugget since 1973, though – previously – he had already been a small shareholder of the New Frontier), an event whose importance will become clear later. The Golden Nugget opened its doors on August 30, 1946 (before the Flamingo on the Strip), and was the brainchild of Guy MacAfee, a former Los Angeles cop who had switched sides, entering the ranks of an organized crime family in Los Angeles. The cost of this casino with no hotel rooms – which would only be added starting in 1977 – is estimated at $ 1,000,000 at the time (equivalent to $ 12,600,000 today). It was here that Steve Wynn and Frank Sinatra first met and then became friends in the 1980s. The gold nugget of more than 27 kilograms displayed in the lobby – the second largest ever pulled from the bowels of the Earth – is traditionally this casino's trademark. It is called "The Hand of Faith", because of its shape reminiscent of a hand, and has a value of approximately $ 1,100,000 at October 2017 prices.

8

THE LEGENDARY FLAMINGO

It is time to tackle an aspect of Las Vegas history that is widely embellished by Hollywood. I am thinking – in particular – of the movie *Bugsy* (released in 1991), the story of the infamous gangster Benjamin 'Bugsy' Siegel, born Siegelbaum. Let's start by saying that Siegel hated his nickname. Who could blame him for this?

Siegel was born in 1906 in Brooklyn, New York City, of poor parents from today's Ukraine, at that time a region of the immense Russian Empire (when the last czar, Nicholas II, still reigned). Quite early he stands out for his marked criminal inclination and accumulates a long list of charges, including robberies, murders and rapes. Over the years, his contacts in the organized crime world include people of the caliber of Al Capone, Charles 'Lucky' Luciano and Frank Costello, the latter two prominent members of the Genovese family. Apart from his life as a gangster, what we care about is Siegel's role in the birth of Las Vegas. Should we believe the screenplay of *Bugsy* and Warren Beatty's spectacular interpretation, Siegel would – more or less – be the real creator and founder of the Strip, as well as of the Flamingo Hotel & Casino.

Actually, that's not true.

Given that it is not possible to identify one "founder" of the city of Las Vegas, being as it is a process of years due to a series of events that are often unconnected with each other, the importance and role of which become obvious only in hindsight, Siegel is not even the creator of the Flamingo. Hollywood needed a character that would appeal to the audience and came up with the tale of Siegel as a dreamer, able to imagine the first true casino hotel where others only saw a desolate wasteland. In point of fact, the creator of the Flamingo is a man named William Richard Wilkerson.

William Wilkerson was a businessman and adventurer (but not a criminal) in Los Angeles, founder of the *Hollywood Reporter* magazine, dedicated to the Hollywood world and all its stories. Thanks to the unscrupulous use of news and above all scandals related to the Studios, this newspaper became a real power center in the world of cinema and a great source of income for Wilkerson, who went on to acquire control over a whole series of hotels and nightclubs in Los Angeles, especially along Sunset Boulevard. But Wilkerson was also a compulsive gambler and he often lost large sums of money at the gaming tables. Until one day, one acquaintance of him decided to make a little joke: the only way to get out of a gambling session as a winner is to be the house. «Build a casino. Own the house.» Wilkerson had the classic light-bulb moment and there and then the true story of the Flamingo began.

Once he decided that it was time to start earning something with gambling, instead of always losing, Wilkerson set out to design and build what was meant to be the most ambitious and luxurious casino hotel ever conceived, to be built – instead of downtown – directly on the Strip (Las Vegas Boulevard South). To this purpose, in January 1944 he bought – from a certain Margaret Folsom – a piece of land of thirty-two acres on which to build his casino, which he paid $ 84,000 (about $ 1,200,000 today).

What Wilkerson had in mind was a proper resort, something never seen before in Las Vegas. He wanted his hotel to be a perfect vacationing place, even for guests not interested in gambling: an extremely innovative concept – almost revolutionary – for the time. Therefore, it was expected that the rooms would be rather welcoming – whereas previously hotel rooms at casino resorts were nothing more than a place to sleep and take a shower, in order to minimize the time spent away from the tables – and the new resort had to offer amenities such as high-end restaurants, quality shows and even outdoor activities. Architects and decorators accustomed to working for Hollywood celebrities were contacted to give life to Wilkerson's dream.

To make it short, by dint of enhancing and bedecking the project, the expenditure forecast reached unsustainable levels for Wilkerson. It was then that one of his acquaintances, Moe Sedway, who ran the El Cortez downtown on behalf of Meyer Lansky – a boss of the organized crime particularly active in the gambling industry – suggested to Wilkerson to bring on board Lansky, in order to secure the necessary funding. At the time, in addition to the El Cortez Lansky did control gambling parlors in Florida, New Orleans and Cuba. Here we can connect to a scene of *The Godfather part II* (one of Francis Ford Coppola's greatest masterpieces, released in 1974): during his visit to Havana (still under the rule of dictator Batista, before Castro took power), Michael Corleone – masterfully played by Al Pacino – meets with Hyman Roth, a fictional character representing Meyer Lansky himself. In the movie, Roth/Lansky talks to Don Corleone about a *protégé* of his, Moe Greene, who did "invent" Las Vegas from nothing. This Moe Greene – also a fictional character – would be no other than Bugsy Siegel. So, in essence, *The Godfather* producers and screenwriters also propose the legend of Siegel founder of Las Vegas and inventor of the Flamingo.

At this point, as one would expect when getting into a partnership with the Mob, Lansky took control of the project and sent Bugsy Siegel to Las Vegas as his lieutenant to supervise the work and to ensure that his instructions were thoroughly followed. Siegel's role in the creation of the Flamingo – therefore – is way less crucial than we are usually told.

The Flamingo Hotel & Casino opened its doors on December 26, 1946, with 105 rooms and was considered the first luxury hotel in Las Vegas. Thanks to the contacts of Wilkerson and Siegel in the golden world of Hollywood, stars of the likes of Clark Gable, Lana Turner, Judy Garland and Joan Crawford attended the inauguration (it should be pointed out that the sources do not agree on the actual presence of such actors). Nonetheless, the first weeks of activity were disastrous and the Flamingo even had to be closed temporarily in January 1947, in order to add some finishing touches to the hotel. The resort did open again in March of the same year, getting mixed results. The final bill for this Strip icon did amount to $ 6,000,000 at the time (about $ 75,000,000 today).

It should be added that the Flamingo, aside from not being Siegel's idea at all, wasn't even the first casino hotel built along the Strip, as opposed to what *Bugsy* would have us believe (just remember the scene of Siegel relieving himself in the middle of the desert). Two casino hotels, as we have seen, had already been built on the same stretch of road: El Rancho Vegas, inaugurated on April 3, 1941, at Sahara Av., and The Last Frontier, inaugurated on October 30, 1942, immediately north of today's Fashion Show Mall.

At this point, it is not entirely clear whether Siegel was killed because of the uncertain success of the Flamingo, or because Lansky and his associates were convinced they were heavily robbed by Siegel during the construction of the resort. Expenses were immediately out of control, and when some incriminating evidence about one of Siegel's employees did pop up, Lansky had no choice but to give the go-ahead for the assassination of his *protégé*. On June 20, 1947, Benjamin 'Bugsy' Siegel was riddled with bullets in his Beverly Hills home.

9

FROM FLAMINGO TO CAESARS PALACE

THUNDERBIRD (1948 – 1992)

The Thunderbird was the fourth casino hotel to open along the Strip, practically across the street from the El Rancho Vegas. At the inauguration, the hotel had 76 rooms and another 170 were soon added. In addition to construction costs – estimated at $ 2,000,000 at the time (about $ 20,000,000 today) – owners Marion Hicks and Clifford Jones (vice-governor of Nevada) also faced a $ 145,000 loss at the craps tables on the first night of operation, worth about $ 1,500,000 today. Nevertheless, the Thunderbird did soon prove to be a success. In 1977 the property was renamed Silverbird, and then in 1982 El Rancho Casino, in memory of the El Rancho Vegas (that had been destroyed by a fire in 1960). The plot which the Thunderbird stood on is now part of the property called Fontainebleau, a mega-resort killed by the Great Recession just a few months before its completion (we are talking about that horrible blue monolith of 3,900 rooms north of the Encore).

DESERT INN (1950 – 2000)

With the Desert Inn, along with many of the

properties of the 1950s, we really enter the myth evoked by the name Las Vegas (I think especially of the Sahara, the Sands, the Dunes). This magnificent casino hotel, inaugurated on April 24, 1950, was conceived by Wilbur Clark (no kinship with the railroad magnate met in the first chapter of this story), the classic entrepreneur with dreams bigger than his finances. So much so that, to complete his plan, he was forced to surrender control to Cleveland's underworld, in the person of Moe Dalitz. Does this sequence of events call to mind anything? I'll help you: Flamingo-Wilkerson-Lansky... History repeats itself.

With 300 rooms – all equipped with air conditioning – it would be for a time the largest and most luxurious hotel in the whole of Nevada. Clark had to settle for a role as a front man, reflected in the original name of the resort, that was "Wilbur Clark's Desert Inn". In 1967, Howard Hughes did buy the property from Dalitz for $ 13 million (about $ 95 million today), giving life to a new era for Las Vegas casinos. Eventually, Steve Wynn would gain ownership of this spectacular resort, buying it in 2000 for $ 270 million (which would be $ 385 million today), after a time as the Sheraton Desert Inn in the 1990s. In its place would rise the Wynn Las Vegas. But that's a story for another chapter.

Meanwhile, an impressive array of stars had performed in the Crystal Showroom of the DI, including: Frank Sinatra (starting with his first appearance ever in Vegas on September 4, 1951), Dean Martin, Tony Bennett (real name Anthony Dominick Benedict), Paul Anka, Jimmy Durante, Dionne Warwick, Wayne Newton, Barry Manilow, Cher, Tina Turner. Hats off to one of the *grandes dames* of the Strip.

SAHARA (1952 – 2011)

To speak of the Sahara, deservedly nicknamed "the jewel of the desert", means recalling the most legendary and fabled part of Strip history. Few other Vegas casino hotels can boast such a load of history, glory and charm. Maybe no one.

The area on which the Sahara would rise was occupied at that time by a bingo parlor. That's right: a bingo parlor in the middle of the Strip (at the northern edge, to be precise), called Club Bingo and opened in 1947 by a Milton Prell. In the early 1950s, Prell decided to take a great leap and, after buying twenty acres of land behind the Club Bingo, began building the Sahara Hotel & Casino. It is not clear from where he got the necessary financing, to the tune of $ 5,500,000 at the time (about $ 51 million today), but I could not find evidence of a tie between Prell and organized crime. Assuming it is not just an informational vacuum, the Sahara could be the only historic Strip resort the Mob bosses could not get control of.

However, on October 7, 1952, the Sahara opened its doors, with 240 rooms (there were 1,720 of them when it closed). The resort's theme is Moroccan-inspired. Sahara's Congo Room, the largest showroom in Las Vegas at the time, did host a true who's who of the most acclaimed entertainers of those years and would compete for more than a decade with Sands' equally celebrated Copa Room. A partial list of artists who performed at the Sahara includes: Marlene Dietrich (paid $ 30,000 a week, or $ 275,000 of today), Mae West, Judy Garland, Frank's Rat Pack, Johnny Carson, Paul Anka, Liza Minnelli, Wayne Newton, The Platters, Bill Cosby, etc. etc.

The Beatles stayed at the Sahara for the short stop in Vegas during their 1964 American tour (with two concerts at the Las Vegas Convention Center), and Cary Grant and Grace Kelly stayed there as well. Once, a truly historic reunion happened at the Congo Room. In 1956, Dean Martin and Jerry Lewis, who had paired for a number of films and shows and were great friends, traumatically split up, probably because of a sort of professional jealousy by Martin towards Lewis. In 1975, Lewis was presenting a show featuring Frank Sinatra when the latter – out of the blue – entered the stage accompanied by Martin. The two old quarrelers, certainly gotten wiser with age, immediately did smooth things over and renewed their friendship forever.

Sahara's doors temporarily closed on May 16, 2011, to reopen on August 23, 2014, under the new SLS Las Vegas sign, after a $ 415 million renovation.

SANDS (1952 – 1996)

For the glorious history of the Copa Room, I refer you to chapter 5. Here I add that even among the public, great names of that era aren't certainly missing: stars of the likes of Audrey Hepburn, Lauren Bacall, Yul Brynner , Kirk Douglas, Elizabeth Taylor could be seen at the tables frequently, enjoying the shows of Frank, Dino and company.

Among the entertainers performing at the Sands, it's worth mentioning at the very least Jimmy Durante, Shirley MacLaine, Marlene Dietrich, Louis Armstrong, Nat King Cole and Wayne Newton. It was at the Sands that Frank Sinatra did marry the enchanting Mia Farrow, who was just twenty years of age at the time and thirty years younger than him (July 19, 1966). This marriage, the third of "Blue Eyes", was to be short-lived: the two broke up two years later.

The Sands was inaugurated on December 15, 1952, and was immediately an amazing success. Initially it had 200 rooms, increased to 715 over the years. After the golden age, from the 1970s this casino hotel was no longer able to compete with the new resorts risen along the Strip and did sadly fall into oblivion. In 1989, Sheldon Adelson took over the property, which would be permanently closed on June 30, 1996, and imploded in November of the same year. In the area once occupied by this Strip gem, now stands the Venetian.

RIVIERA (1955 – 2015)

The Riviera opened to the public on April 20, 1955, and – after being relegated for years in an absolutely marginal position compared to the modern Strip giants – it was forced to close its doors on May 4, 2015. Already in 2010 the owners had declared bankruptcy, in order to reorganize its finances according to Chapter 11 bankruptcy law. But the fate of this undoubtedly iconic casino hotel was sealed. Having cost $ 10 million ($ 91 million today) for 291 rooms, thanks to a series of expansions it had meanwhile reached the remarkable number of 2,100 rooms. It was imploded between June and August 2016.

DUNES (1955 – 1993)

The Dunes was inaugurated on May 23, 1955, a month after the Riviera, with 200 rooms. The theme was "Arab Desert". Already in the 1980s, this casino hotel proved not to be up to the challenge, and had to declare bankruptcy in 1984 (but continuing to operate). On January 26, 1993, the Dunes was permanently closed by Steve Wynn – the new owner – to be subsequently imploded. In its place would rise the Bellagio (1998).

HACIENDA (1956 – 1996)

In June 1956, the Hacienda was inaugurated (with 256 rooms initially), a casino hotel that did not leave any major traces in Vegas's history. Located at the southernmost end of the Strip, it would be closed on December 1, 1996, and imploded on New Year's Eve, live on the KTNV TV channel as part of the celebrations. Only in fabulous Las Vegas! Today, in its place you find the Mandalay Bay.

TROPICANA (1957 – still open)

At the time of its opening, the Tropicana was a very ambitious project, complete with a Country Club with an attached golf course – in an area now occupied by the immense property of the MGM Grand – and was perhaps the first attempt to raise the bar compared to the glorious casino hotels of the recent past (mostly the Desert Inn and the Sahara). The Trop was inaugurated on April 3, 1957, with 300 rooms (soon to be 450), costing $ 15 million at the time ($ 131 million today), and still stands in its original location with its two white towers – built in the 1980s – of 1,500 rooms in all. It has to be added that the whole property has recently been renovated at the not insignificant cost of $ 165 million and presents itself – today – in a shape it had not enjoyed for a long time.

STARDUST (1958 – 2006)

It is impossible to close the 1950s chapter (Las Vegas's heyday) without a closer look at the Stardust. The Stardust was a true Strip icon for a long time, in addition to being the forerunner of all the mega-resorts

43

that came. First of all, at the inauguration (July 2, 1958), this was the largest hotel in the world – a record the modern Strip casino hotels would strive to best in the decades to come –, with 1,065 rooms. Additionally, it was perhaps the last of which the bosses of the Mob managed to obtain uncontested control, making it the protagonist of epic clashes with the authorities, recreated – in part – in Martin Scorsese's *Casino* (please check chapter 4).

The Stardust Resort & Casino originated from an idea of Antonio Cornero Stralla, who was born in Italy (in the Piedmontese province of Cuneo in 1899) and immigrated to the United States with his parents after his father had lost everything, partly due to gambling losses and partly because of a fire. Cornero honed his craft during the Prohibition era (like so many of his "colleagues", dare I say it). Subsequently, he threw himself into the gambling industry, including two small ships used as casinos in international waters off the coast of California. Cornero, by then known as Tony 'The Hat' Cornero, would die in disputed circumstances – perhaps poisoned – on July 31, 1955, without being able to see his dream on the Strip realized. Moe Dalitz and Meyer Lansky – ubiquitous figures in those years – took over the project and brought it to completion, thanks to their vast financial resources, obviously of unlawful provenance.

The theme of the resort was the space, and its six separate buildings were called Mars, Mercury, Venus,

Saturn, Jupiter and Neptune. Despite being huge, this hotel was built like a motel, with car parking placed directly in front of their respective rooms. The Lido de Paris show was the main attraction. The story of Frank 'Lefty' Rosenthal – who was in charge of the property on behalf of the Mob (until 1976 out in the open, then until the early 1980s behind the scenes) – and Tony 'The Ant' Spilotro is very well told in *Casino*. Here I add that Spilotro, after creating a gang called "The hole in the wall gang", responsible for many rapes, robberies and any kind of violence in Las Vegas, signed his own death sentence with behavior of the sort his bosses could not appreciate, because it drew too much attention to their profitable activity. Spilotro would end assassinated in 1986 together with his brother Michael.

Undoubtedly, once the epic of the Stardust had come to an end, the Strip would never be the same again. The resort was definitively closed on November 1, 2006, and imploded in March 2007 to make room for the mega-project (similar in scope to the City Center further south) called Echelon Place, before the Great Recession stopped everything indefinitely.

RECAP

The Stardust concludes the systematic presentation of resorts opened along the Strip in the 1940s and 1950s. We got to know them all, beginning with the first one (El Rancho Vegas, completely destroyed by a fire in 1960). Of the twelve we have described, only three still stand in 2017 (Flamingo, Sahara, Tropicana), albeit completely different from how they were initially built: twenty or thirty-story towers did replace two or three-story motel buildings of the past. The Sahara, closed in 2011, reopened in 2014 as SLS Las Vegas, after a thorough renovation.

Between 1958 and 1966, no noteworthy casino hotel was inaugurated on the Strip. We can mention the motel La Concha (the shell), opened in 1961 next to the Riviera, for its eccentric architectural choices, and the Flamingo Capri inaugurated in 1959, which would become the Imperial Palace in 1979 and is now The Linq, but nothing more. From now on, we shall meet a number of characters who, since 1966, have (re)made Las Vegas great. Bold men, who have transformed their daring dreams of greatness into reality, laying the foundations of the Strip that every contemporary visitor gets to know. Many of the "creatures" (as I'm sure they would consider them) of these builders of fairy-tale palaces are still part of the Vegas skyline, nowadays often surrounded by hotels even more colossal. We are about to abandon a stage of the past that no longer exists, to enter another one that is an integral part of the Strip's present. Enjoy the ride!

10

JAY SARNO AND THE CAESARS PALACE

«You can get an argument over who started the Las Vegas Strip, but there's no question it was Jay Sarno who changed it forever.» (*Las Vegas Review Journal*, February 7, 1999).

It is really impossible to overestimate the impact this chubby and energetic man has had on Vegas's history. At the time, in the first half of the 1960s, the casino hotels built or managed by the Mob – that were so instrumental in creating the Las Vegas myth – were old and no longer able to excite anyone. Their themes (the Far West, Arabia, Morocco, the Tropics, the Côte d'Azur, space) were superficially executed and unimaginative. Not only that: for the first time in history, the immense American middle class began to have money to spend that was not indispensable for everyday needs and thus available for discretionary spending. I remind you that – in the previous two decades – Strip casinos were mostly attended by people from the upper echelons of the income scale, who liked to show up dressed in tuxedos and evening gowns at the various restaurants and clubs. Any player of limited means was immediately labeled as vicious and irresponsible.

But now we are at the beginning of the cultural revolution that will be remembered as "the '68" and everything is going to change. Andy Warhol is introducing Americans and the world to a different way of looking at reality. In 1962 he had exhibited in New York his "Marilyn Diptych", considered by many critics one of the ten most important works of modern art. The Beatles are changing the history of pop music.

This is the context that saw Jay Sarno bursting on the scene with all his energy. He was born in 1922 to working class parents who, however, managed to send him to the University of Missouri to study Economics. There he met Stanley Mallin, who became his best friend and business partner for life. Both fought in the Pacific Theater during World War II, and then became tight associates when the war ended. After a time as tile vendors and installers in Miami and another period as building contractors in Atlanta, the two tried their luck in the motel sector. Sarno had some (limited) experience in the field, thanks to a few summer months – during his juvenile years – spent assisting his brother, who owned a small hotel. The first Cabana Motel rose in Atlanta and was successful enough to allow Sarno and Mallin to expand the business, opening a second one in Dallas and a third one in Palo Alto. But Sarno, who – as a passionate gambler – often stopped in Vegas to play the games, soon realized that he could earn much more money with a single casino hotel than with a whole chain of motels. In 1961, he decided that this would be his way.

In 1962, a meeting took place that would change Sarno's life forever and, in hindsight, the future of the Strip. It was when Sarno and Mallin became acquainted with Jimmy Hoffa, the powerful head of the International Brotherhood of Teamsters (or just Teamsters), the rather pretentious name chosen by the workers' union representing drivers, bellboys, handymen and other workers without particular qualifications. The power of Hoffa, who would lead the union from 1958 to 1971, came from the money accumulated in the pension fund of the unionized workers, which Hoffa managed virtually to his liking. One of his favorite investments was lending to entrepreneurs willing to open casinos in Las Vegas, including those with less than reputable backgrounds. No bank, in those years, was willing to finance the construction of casino hotels and Hoffa became – to all intents and purposes – the man all the operators interested in a share of Las Vegas action were forced to turn to. Sarno was well aware of that and, therefore, knew he needed to convince Hoffa to finance his dream project.

Hoffa immediately took a liking to Sarno: the two men were cut from the same cloth. But, being a skilled businessman, he demanded that Sarno and Mallin – with no experience in the casino industry – only come back to him if they were able to involve in the project a partner with broader shoulders than theirs, financially speaking. So, Sarno and Mallin convinced Nathan Jacobson, an acquaintance of Sarno who had already become wealthy thanks to his insurance business, to join the endeavor and – towards the end of 1962 – they got access to Hoffa's funds.

Sarno, as you would expect, had in mind something truly impressive, capable of crushing any competition active at the time on the Strip. Mediocrity just wasn't his cup of tea. His stated goal was to create a real palace of luxuries and pleasures, where every customer could feel like an emperor for a day or two. The name Caesars Palace was thus born, as he himself later explained: not the palace of one Caesar (which would have required the insertion of the apostrophe before the s, as in Caesar's Palace), but the palace of all Caesars, for anyone, any customer that is, ought to feel like a Caesar (or Cleopatra). He insisted his architect, Jo Harris (a woman), put a flood of statues, columns, capitals, busts and fountains in the building, in order to create a representation – more or less faithful – of how Sarno and the American public imagined Ancient Rome. The Caesars Palace thus became the first example of "entertainment architecture", an architecture designed to amaze and engage the visitor in a new and certainly more intense visual experience than normal. It was no longer just the content to amuse and entertain (the casino and the shows), but the container itself, i.e. the building with its architecture. Entering the Caesars Palace meant getting in a different dimension, leaving everyday life behind. The Strip's future was sealed.

Faithful to his character, for the inauguration of the new resort Sarno organized three days of uninterrupted celebrations (August 5-7, 1966). Gorgeous half-naked models welcomed the most important guests with the inscription "I am your slave" and Champagne flowed freely. Lobsters, caviar and filet mignon sated the hunger of 1,800 invited VIP guests. Caesars Palace's inauguration made the news all over the country, even on TV. Nothing like that had ever been attempted before. Sarno himself always enjoyed life to the fullest: from the gambling (heavy), to the pretty ladies (many), to the pleasures of the palate, this man has always lived in the fast lane. When he played golf, he liked to bet $ 15,000 per hole (about $ 113,000 in 2017). When his wife Joyce complained about his countless affairs, he gave her a fur coat, a diamond or a new car to calm her down. This would not, however, be enough to avoid divorce, which happened in 1974.

The more reliable estimates concerning the cost of this casino hotel speak of $ 25 million at the time ($ 190 million today), a figure never before approached, of which one million (about $ 7,500,000 today) just for expenses related to the lavish inauguration. There was enough to make the investors very nervous, but the new resort – as expected by Sarno – soon turned out to be an unmatched money machine. The staff in charge of counting the cash coming from the gaming tables had to begin to weigh the money, because counting it would take too long. The Caesars – moreover – became a real boxing Mecca and all the most important boxing matches of the 1970s and 1980s took place there. Muhammad Ali (Cassius Clay), Sugar Ray Leonard, Thomas Hearns, Larry Holmes and many other great boxers fought at the Caesars.

To the original Roman Tower (14 floors for 680 rooms) the Centurion Tower and Forum Tower were soon added. More recently, as further proof of the immortal success of the Caesars Palace (now the crown jewel of Caesars Entertainment Corporation, formerly Harrah's Entertainment), three much bigger towers have been built, which today define this resort: the 1,100-room Palace Tower in August 1997, the Augustus Tower (900 rooms, on the south side of the property, near the Strip) and the Octavius Tower, inaugurated in January 2012 (665 rooms, on the south side as well, but located farther from the Strip). Someone may find this detailed information about the different towers of a hotel tedious, but – as the more experienced visitors know – it is almost always desirable to stay in the most recently built rooms, which are usually more spacious, more modern and less worn than older ones, unless the latter have undergone a substantial renovation. In short, tower after tower, the Caesars Palace has become one of the largest hotels in the world, counting today almost 4,000 rooms in all.

Of course, this is where Dustin Hoffman and Tom Cruise did win big at the blackjack tables, thanks to the extraordinary card counting skills of Hoffman's character, landing one of the most spectacular penthouse suites on the Strip, rigorously comped (*Rain Man*, 1988). And let's not forget it was in Caesars' imposing lobby that Zach Galifianakis's character did ask if Caesar lived there, meaning the Roman consul and dictator himself (*The Hangover*, 2009). Well, no, he did not!

Sarno's second project was definitely less lucky. Being the basically immature guy he was, Sarno thought that a casino strongly inspired by a circus-like setting could attract a large number of gamblers who, in his opinion, would have the time of their life gambling surrounded by clowns, jugglers, trapeze artists and even... animals. That was how the Circus Circus was born, inaugurated on October 18, 1968, with the look of a gigantic circus tent. Contrary to what one would suppose, therefore, the Circus Circus was not conceived as a family resort, but just as a casino. Sarno's mistake, however, was twofold: the number of adults willing to play blackjack, craps or roulette in a circus-like environment (and chaos) was far inferior to what he expected and – inexplicably – the Circus Circus opened as a casino without hotel rooms. This huge strategic mistake made Sarno's second venture on the Strip a failure.

As if that were not enough, in 1969 the FBI task force responsible for cleansing Las Vegas from organized crime accused Caesars' financial manager, Jerome Zarowitz, of having links with the Genovese Mob family, specifically with Anthony 'Fat Tony' Salerno. Zarowitz, moreover, had already been in jail for a crime related to illegal betting. Following a well-established technique, the feds "convinced" Sarno, Mallin and Jacobson to sell the Caesars Palace in order to avoid more serious consequences. The three partners – already struggling to fix the Circus Circus – did sell without too many regrets, in part because they got $ 60 million ($ 400 million today) for the property, over twice as much as the resort had cost. That's the story of how Sarno, one of Vegas's greatest visionaries of all time, lost control over his most brilliant project within just three years.

Now free to focus on their second venture, the three partners realized how urgent it was to add a hotel to the Circus Circus casino. In 1972, the first tower of 400 rooms was inaugurated, called the Casino Tower (the lowest tower just behind the casino). Despite all his efforts, Sarno soon lost control of his second project too. On the one hand, the Circus Circus never became profitable, and – just as had happened a few years earlier with the Caesars Palace – the FBI also targeted this resort. The reason for such doggedness was not Sarno himself, who had no connection with the Mob, but a certain Tony 'The Ant' Spilotro. For those who don't remember him, please refer to chapter 4. Spilotro, firmly determined to manage his criminal activities in Vegas, had been able to get the concession for a gift shop inside the Circus Circus, using his mother's maiden name. It seems that Sarno had no idea who Spilotro was, but his mere presence was enough for the FBI to compel the three partners to sell the Circus Circus as well, making use of the strategy so successful in the past. It's 1974, and in just eight years' time Sarno had built and then lost two of the most iconic and significant casino hotels in Strip history. The Circus Circus would later become the first family resort, under the leadership of new owners Bill Bennett and Bill Pennington. But that's another story for another day.

Jay Sarno would die of heart attack in 1984, only 62 years old, in a suite of his beloved Caesars Palace, of course. The project he was working on – appropriately called 'Grandissimo' (which means 'very big' in Italian) – had not found any backers. Perhaps because, with 6,000 rooms and an estimated $ 1 billion price tag ($ 2,5 billion in 2017 dollars), it was really too much of everything for the 1980s Strip. And so ends the short but very intense adventure of Jay Sarno in Vegas. The traces left by this hopeless dreamer are still very well visible along the Strip, not only in the two resorts he has conceived and built, but also in all those born in the following thirty years. Sarno's legacy, in this sense, truly is immortal.

11

HOWARD HUGHES, THE MAN WHO BOUGHT LAS VEGAS

On the evening of November 24, 1966, a man arrived in Las Vegas by private train, traveled down the Strip in a car, occupied the entire top floor of the Desert Inn – where the high roller suites were located – with his staff and set about to change the face of the city forever. His name was Howard Robard Hughes Jr.

At the time, Howard Hughes was considered one of the richest men in the world. Gambling, though, was not one of his pastimes. So much so that the management of the DI, in anticipation of the huge turnover expected as usual for the end of the year, repeatedly asked him to clear the suites. Not at all impressed and indeed quite a bit annoyed, Hughes – who did not like to obey orders – bought the entire hotel. He paid $ 13.5 million for it, corresponding to $ 102 million in 2017 dollars. Not a figure to lose any sleep over for a man who had just collected $ 564.5 million (nearly $ 4.3 billion today) from the sale of TWA, the glorious Trans World Airlines born in 1925, which would be taken over by American Airlines in 2001. Actually, it seems that the enormous liquidity resulting from the sale of TWA was the main reason for the long series of investments of Hughes in Las Vegas, made – most likely – to get substantial tax deductions on the newly generated profits.

Whatever the motivation of Hughes, in just four years this eccentric billionaire put his hands on following Sin City properties: the Sands, the Castaways (a casino hotel opened in 1963 in the area now occupied by the Mirage), the New Frontier, the Silver Slipper (a casino without hotel rooms opened in 1950 right next to the Last Frontier, New Frontier from 1955) and the Landmark (I will talk about it shortly). Hughes's total investment in those years amounted to about $ 65 million (about $ 480 million today) and – at the end of this incredible acquisition ride – Hughes managed to own 20% of all the available rooms on the Strip, in addition to vast plots of land. One of those would become the Master Planned Community of Summerlin, about ten miles west of downtown (Summerlin was one of Hughes's grandmothers).

Hughes's biography and personality were the complete opposite of Sarno's: born rich – his father had patented an innovative two-cone roller bit that allowed oil to be extracted from previously inaccessible layers –, he was a maniac of secrecy and over the years he did develop, apparently, an "obsessive-compulsive disorder". This would result in a long list of manic behaviors, including his obsession with cleanliness and hygiene, as well as with the size of peas. Certainly, among his compulsions there was no place for gambling or women, unlike *bon vivant* Jay Sarno. Hughes had basically two passions: aviation and cinema.

In his role as a film producer, Hughes produced a number of successful movies in the 1920s and 1930s, including the first *Scarface* (1932). As an aviator, he established several world records and founded the Hughes Aircraft Company, which became an important supplier of the US Department of Defense during World War II. But let's examine the impact Hughes had on Las Vegas.

It has to be noted that Hughes had no interest at all in the casino industry: his presence in Vegas was justified – on the one hand – by his willingness to immediately reinvest part of the profits deriving from the sale of his stake in the TWA company (which he had taken control of in 1939), to save on taxes. His other motivation – we could argue – was to be the biggest fish of all in a relatively small pond instead of just a big fish in a giant pond such as the State of California and the national scene. Hughes did like to have a certain influence on politicians who were in a position to favor or hinder his business ventures, and this result was certainly easier to achieve in a small state that was almost totally dependent on casino revenues rather than in California or even Washington. The fact that Nevada did not have (as is still the case) any personal income tax was undeniably a factor as well.

Hughes's role in the explosive development the Strip would experience in the decades to follow – more than ever starting in 1989 – was indirect and would only become apparent over the years. In 1955, Nevada's governing bodies decided it was time to centralize licensing and control over licenses assigned to casino owners and managers in the state, until then in the hands of the sheriff's office, easily subject to outside pressures and corruption. Keep in mind that in the 1940s and 1950s, the Mob owned virtually all Vegas casino hotels. The new rules, finally implemented with some strictness, provided that every single co-owner, as well as every single manager with executive responsibility within a casino, got – in order to operate – a special authorization from the expressly created Gaming Control Board: a License. People with a criminal record or of questionable associations were easily excluded.

Hughes himself, in theory, should not have been allowed to receive the necessary license, because he was categorically refusing to leave his suite and to meet personally with the Board's commission, an indispensable step to initiate the licensing process. The governor of the state, Paul Laxalt, intervened to ensure that Hughes did not encounter any problems. The power of money, of course, but also foresight on Laxalt's part. The governor understood that Hughes could become a perfect solution to the problem of the Mob presence in Las Vegas: every casino bought by

Hughes meant one casino less in the hands of organized crime. Additionally, the arrival on the scene of a reputable and well-known businessman such as Hughes – this was Laxalt's reasoning – would greatly increase Vegas's respectability in the eyes of the average American and – as a result – its appeal as a vacation spot. He was right.

The problem with this process of licensing was that corporations (such as the big companies listed on the stock exchange) were in fact excluded from any Las Vegas investment, since it would be unthinkable to submit each individual shareholder to the authorization process. This was a clear limit to the development of the Strip, because only large corporations would be able to provide the capital needed to create the mega-resorts that today illuminate every inch of it.

All this changed forever in 1969, when the Nevada Assembly approved the Corporate Gaming Act, a law limiting the need to obtain a license from the Gaming Control Board to shareholders owning at least 5% of the shares of corporations owning casinos, in addition to managers at executive level. The law was also given retroactive validity to July 1, 1967. The way for the entry of large listed companies on the Strip was paved. Barron Hilton, chairman of the hotel chain bearing his name, would be the first to take advantage of it, taking over – a few years later – the Flamingo and the International from Kirk Kerkorian, another magnate we'll get to know.

Howard Hughes left Las Vegas as secretly as when he arrived, on the night of November 25, 1970. He would die six years later. At the time of his death, his personal fortune would amount to about $ 2.5 billion, equivalent to about $ 11 billion today. During four unrepeatable years, and almost unintentionally, this mysterious and mentally suffering man had left an indelible mark on Strip's history, planting the seeds of the incredible development yet to come.

12

THE LANDMARK HOTEL & CASINO

The Landmark, mentioned in the previous chapter, deserves a brief description. Conceived by a certain Frank Carroll in the early 1960s, the Landmark had a troubled history, because the money ended long before the necessary work: a recurring curse in Las Vegas. The construction of the tower, which began in 1961, had to be suspended in December 1962 for lack of funds. Since then, the Landmark – 80% complete – would lay abandoned for four years. In 1966, thanks to a further loan from the Teamsters, the work resumed... only to be interrupted again in 1967, shortly before inauguration day. Again, at the last minute the necessary funds were missing. Howard Hughes bought the property – virtually finished – in January 1969, paying it $ 17.3 million (corresponding to $ 115 million today), an amount that includes what was due to the various creditors involved.

The Landmark did open to the public in July of the same year and did leave a trace more than anything because of its original architecture, based on a mushroom-shaped tower of 31 floors, which – at the time – was the highest in all of Nevada. More than half of the 525 rooms were located inside the tower, while the rest were in the usual motel-style buildings common to all Strip casino hotels. The Landmark did resist until 1990, despite being permanently in serious financial difficulties, and did bow out in spectacular fashion: in 1995 it was imploded by the "Martians" (for Tim Burton's *Mars Attacks!*, released in 1996).

13

KIRK KERKORIAN, BUILDER OF GIANTS

Kerkor 'Kirk' Kerkorian perfectly embodies the American Dream, meaning the chance for anyone, if equipped with sufficient spirit of enterprise and a bit of luck, to achieve results – in terms of financial and personal satisfaction – unthinkable in other places.

Kerkorian, born on June 15, 1917, in California to parents of Armenian origin, has been a decisive player in shaping the Strip we all know. It is no coincidence if he has been called the "father of the mega-resort": we shall see that it's a more than deserved title. The life of this man was adventurous to say the least, worthy of a Hollywood blockbuster.

Having dropped out of school after eighth grade, he initially took advantage of his remarkable body size to become a boxer of some success. Towards the end of the 1930s, realizing that the world was soon to be at war and wanting at all costs to avoid to serve in the infantry, he decided to become a pilot. To pay for his flying lessons, he agreed to take care of the small herd of his instructor, Florence 'Pancho' Barnes, one of the first female pilots ever. Translation: he cleaned the stable and milked the cows.

The sacrifice of those months, however, bore abundant fruit: at the outbreak of World War II, the British needed a lot of aircraft built in Canada, the Mosquito from de Havilland. The journey over the North Atlantic was extremely dangerous: the aircraft's range was just enough to reach the Scottish coast and the losses – in terms of planes and pilots – outnumbered the successful crossings. But the reward for the ones who made it was impressive: $ 1,000 for each airplane delivered. Within two and a half years, Kerkorian piloted 33 Mosquitos to Britain on behalf of the Royal Air Force, bringing home – apart from his own skin – the equivalent of over half a million dollars today. A small capital from which to start building what would become a great empire.

Kerkorian's first investment in Las Vegas, in 1962, was to buy 80 acres of land on the Strip, just across the street from the Flamingo. It would be on this plot of land that – four years later – the Caesars Palace would rise. In 1967, Kerkorian doubled down, using the profits from his previous deal to buy an 82-acre plot along Paradise Road. Right there, with the help of architect Martin Stern Jr., Kerkorian did build his first casino hotel: the International Hotel (later Las Vegas Hilton). Always in 1967, in order to gain experience and to adequately train the personnel that would be needed two years later to staff the International, Kerkorian also took over the ownership of the history-laden Flamingo.

On the date of its inauguration on July 30, 1969, the International was the largest hotel in the world, and we shall see how this would become a constant in Kerkorian's Las Vegas career. It cost $ 80 million at the time ($ 535 million 2017), an astonishing amount for a hotel. Barbra Streisand was the star of the inaugural evening, followed by a certain Elvis Presley, who at the International would crown his explosive career with a series of never forgotten shows: 58 sold outs in a row, praised by audiences and critics in equal measure. In the second showroom of the hotel, meanwhile, the musical *Hair* was getting great reviews too. It almost seemed to be back in Vegas's golden era, the fabulous 1950s we've celebrated earlier.

It is worth reporting what was published by *The Daily Telegraph* in London on the day of Stern's death in 2001: «The International, whose triform 30-floor tower contained 1,519 rooms, became the most imitated building on the Las Vegas Strip: it provided the model for the Bellagio, Treasure Island, Mirage and Mandalay Bay, among other hotels.» Not a minor role, as you can see.

But Kerkorian had even bigger projects. In 1969, he had already gained control over the famed Metro-Goldwyn-Mayer (MGM) film studios at a favorable price due to the studios' financial difficulties at the time. Kerkorian was more interested in the prestige of the brand and in the real estate of the company than in the production of movies. In order to fund his new venture, in 1970 Kerkorian sold both the International and the Flamingo to the Hilton group. The Hilton Hotels Corporation subsequently expanded the hotel in a clever way: it simply added a piece to two of the three towers it was made of, without tearing down anything and giving the building an irregular shape. An inexpensive and functional idea. Elvis, incidentally, did stay for years at the Las Vegas Hilton, to the point of earning a commemorative statue that is still there.

For the first time in Las Vegas's history, a stock-listed corporation with thousands of shareholders appeared on the Strip and took control of a number of casinos, something unthinkable only a few years earlier. Vegas really had got ahead a lot since the era of Bugsy Siegel and the various Mob "families"!

In 1972, MGM announced that it would undertake a massive diversification: it would build, along the Strip of course, the largest casino hotel in the world. Said and done: on December 5, 1973, the MGM Grand was inaugurated – which today is the Bally's – with no less than 2,084 rooms spread over 26 floors. As promised, it was at the time the largest hotel in the world (and that makes two for Kerkorian). It cost $ 107 million, or about $ 590 million today. The name of the resort was inspired by a famous MGM movie of 1932: *Grand Hotel*. It might be worth recollecting the parade of movie stars that had performed in that film: Greta Garbo, Joan Crawford, John Barrymore (Drew

Barrymore's grandfather), among others.

On November 21, 1980, a terrible tragedy struck this Strip behemoth and the whole city: one of the deadliest fires in US history took place at the MGM Grand, leaving 85 people dead and at least 400 injured. The fire's causes were carefully investigated and brought – as you would expect – to modify the fire regulations for Vegas hotels. In particular, the inquiry came to the conclusion that the fire had originated in one of the many resort restaurants, due to an electrical failure. A problem that would have been easily manageable without major damage had become a deadly nightmare due to an article of fire regulations that excluded from the obligation to install a sprinkler system all the areas of the building that required the presence of people twenty-four hours a day. That's because it was assumed that – with someone on site – the alarm for a nascent fire would be given immediately. So the casino and the resort cafeteria open 24/7 – every Las Vegas hotel has one – were excluded from the obligation to install fire sprinklers in the ceiling. Unfortunately, MGM's had just changed opening times and was deserted at night.

The fire broke out in the early hours of the morning (the fire department got their first call at 7:17) and this prevented the alarm from being given promptly. The hotel's construction technique, moreover, included a number of air ducts that went from the ground floor up to the higher floors and fueled the catastrophe. The vast majority of deaths, in fact, were due to the suffocating smoke – more than half of the victims died in an attempt to escape from the stairs – and to the very dangerous carbon monoxide that always accompanies fires. Colorless and odorless, this silent killer left 25 of the 85 victims directly in the rooms, dead without even realizing what was happening.

In the aftermath of this tragedy, no less than 1,327 lawsuits were brought by hotel guests and family members of victims against 118 different companies. A compensation fund was created, endowed with $ 223 million ($ 590 million today, equivalent to the building costs of the entire casino hotel seven years earlier). Eight months after the fire, the MGM Grand did reopen its doors, completely renovated and – obviously – with the latest fire fighting systems installed. The foolish norm that allowed the spreading of the flames, it goes without saying, had been amended in the meantime.

In 1986, Kerkorian sold his two MGM Grand resorts (the second was in Reno, Nevada) to Bally Manufacturing Corp., which produced pinball machines and slot machines. And so the Bally's Las Vegas that we still know today was born. That doesn't mean, however, that he had decided to pull out of Las Vegas: on December 18, 1993, Kerkorian once again opened the world's largest hotel (it's three now) with the name – *repetita iuvant* – of MGM Grand. At a cost of $ 1.1 billion (and we move on, from millions to billions), equal to nearly $ 1.9 billion 2017, the green behemoth of 30 floors – for 5,005 total rooms – that all visitors to Sin City can admire at the intersection of the Strip with Tropicana Av. was inaugurated. It is quite obvious that the "families" of organized crime would never have been able to provide such sums of money to fund the construction of new resorts, even if the authorities hadn't forcefully thrown them out of Vegas over the previous decades. The big banks, now convinced of the legality and the decency of the casino business, had in the meantime embarked without further ado in this new (for them) adventure.

The importance of this resort is such that it deserves a brief introduction in a dedicated chapter, also because it is part of a later and different era of Strip history. During his long career as an investor, Kerkorian was also active in other sectors of the economy: I especially think of the big automakers, who came to fear his infamous raids. But that's another story.

14

WHALES AND MILLIONS

We'll now meet one of Las Vegas's (and the world's) most legendary gamblers. But, first, a brief explanation.

Las Vegas was born as a dormitory village at the time of the construction of the railroad that was to connect Los Angeles to Salt Lake City (as we learned in the first chapter of this book) and it got bigger and bigger, as we all know, thanks to profits generated by gambling and to a clever management of Vegas's place in the collective imagination. The catch phrase «What happens in Vegas, stays in Vegas» (with its variant «What happens here, stays here»), just to give you an example, was coined in 2003 by the R & R Partners advertising agency on behalf of the Las Vegas Convention and Visitors Authority and was unintentionally brought to the national attention – where it would stay to this day – by no less than Laura Bush, president George W. Bush's wife. In 2004, the First Lady answered a question from TV host Jay Leno with the now famous phrase during an interview on *The Tonight Show*. This lucky slogan best defines the real reason behind the ongoing success of this city: a vacation in the deeper sense of the word is what Las

Vegas promises you, from the Latin verb *vacare*, which means being free of... (commitments, timetables, responsibility), having spare time for... (games, fun, various transgressions).

Although table games and slot machine revenues now only account for 34.24% of total revenues for resorts along the Strip (2016 data), and 49.34% for the downtown area – that doesn't have the luxury hotels, the starred restaurants and the Cirque du Soleil shows crowding the Strip –, it seems to me that observers who comment on these statistics as an unmistakable sign of the now marginal importance of gambling in the general economy of the city are missing two decisive facts:

1. Without the profits generated by the casino industry, it would never have been possible to build the mega-resorts that attract millions of tourists today, thanks to their restaurants, shops, shows, nightclubs and spas.

2. Although the gambling budget per visitor has not increased for years, and stays at around $ 600 on average (after going down during the Great Recession), and although there is certainly a part of visitors who don't put one single dollar in a slot machine (31% of all visitors in 2016), I strongly doubt that Las Vegas would be chosen by the millions of tourists visiting it annually – a record 43 million in 2016 – if it became a generic "fun city", devoid of casinos.

Even today, the gambling component – in my

opinion – remains absolutely crucial to ensuring the city's success (and survival).

Let's come to the real topic of this chapter: the "whales".

You should know that – inside the casinos – there is a real ranking of all guests/players based on how much the casino hopes to make from each one, according to very accurate calculations. Summarizing: if you are a blackjack player betting $ 50 on average for each hand and you usually spend three hours each night at your favorite table, the casino can calculate that your overall gaming volume, referred to as *churn*, will amount to about $ 9,000 daily ($ 50 x 60 hands/h x 3 h), for a *hold* or *drop* – the casino's profit based on the mathematical advantage given to it by the rules applied to the game – of $ 180, if a statistical average of 2% house advantage is used. Of this theoretical profit of $ 180, the casino is willing to return 25% to 40% to the player, i.e. $ 45-72, depending on your relationship with the various floormen and with your host, whether you are a regular customer or not, etc. Figures and percentages may vary, but the operating principle is the one described, provided you are a *rated* player, which means that your play is evaluated (you must have a card, often called *comp card*, to be handed to the floorman whenever you sit down at a table).

Obviously, you won't get cash, but so-called comps (for complimentaries): line pass for the buffet or disco (used to jump the line), room discounts, tickets for some show, up to large suites completely free. The system is definitely fascinating and the possibilities for casinos to reward their most affluent customers virtually limitless, especially in this era of mega-resorts.

As we have seen, the casinos rank all players according to their importance, that is, according to their gaming volume. At the base of the pyramid we find the masses, made of players placing bets that are too small to make them eligible for the various gifts available. Slightly above them, there are the serious players that the casino knows and does not want to lose, who can hope to get occasional invitations to spend a few days at the property free of charge (keep in mind that the hotel rooms are the least onerous freebies for the resort itself, even when "worth" $ 200-300 a night, unless it's full house). Higher yet in status are the *high rollers*, which are extremely important for the casino economy. These customers are accustomed to betting from a minimum of $ 500 to a few thousand dollars per hand, whether it's blackjack, craps, baccarat or roulette, and often have a $ 100,000 to $ 500,000 line of credit at the casino. At the very top of the pyramid, in the Olympus of gambling, we find the *whales*, so called because of their incredible "size".

Here we are talking about multimillionaires, sometimes even billionaires, who – gripped by the demon of gambling – can literally change the fate of the quarterly earnings report of a big casino, for better or worse. We must not forget that, despite the fact that the casino maintains an insurmountable mathematical advantage in the long run, in the short run and for the single player everything is possible. Even winning millions. The Gaussian curve (distribution of probabilities) explains why. Consequently, these gamblers of almost limitless means are as coveted as they are feared by casinos all over the world. Feared above all if they are sufficiently disciplined to go away with a big win, instead of playing long enough to lose again everything and maybe something more.

The most legendary of them all was, most likely, Kerry Packer (December 17, 1937 – December 26, 2005). An Australian media tycoon and inveterate gambler, with a personal fortune estimated at US $ 5 billion in the 1990s, this man was so wealthy that he had fun sending shivers of fear down the back of the many casino managers and owners he loved to challenge. Packer was able to ruin – on his own – the quarterly report of a gambling corporation, which he enjoyed a lot. Of course, just as often he was the source of big profits for the casinos he attended. As in 1999, when he lost 11 million pounds in a London casino playing blackjack, the biggest payout ever recorded by a casino in the UK.

Packer's trait as a gambler that made him so feared was his discipline: he was able to quit the gaming table at any time, whether he was winning or losing millions. And, because of the math advantage that – in the long run – always rewards the house, the casinos hate gamblers who leave with money in their pockets. Luckily for Vegas, there are really few of them.

Packer, as well as being one of the greatest gamblers of all time, usually gave princely tips to the casino employees where he played, thus becoming their darling. His favorite pastime was to bet the maximum allowed in a certain casino, then ask to raise the limit. When he was told that no, that would not be possible, he was over the moon.

On March 31, 1992, Kerry Packer set up at the Caesars Palace and began – as usual – to play at the highest limits. Apparently, from the late 1980s Packer had a credit line of $ 5 million (about $ 10 million today) at Caesars, the highest ever granted in Strip history. At midnight he was up $ 9 million, and Caesars World's quarterly profit (the corporation owning the casino at the time) was cut by 50% for the first quarter, which closes on March 31. By dawn, Packer had lost again all the previously accumulated winnings, plus a couple million of his own. Caesars World's second quarter financial accounts were resurrected!

One morning in 1995, he appeared at the MGM Grand casino, claiming a whole blackjack pit (a group of tables assembled to form a kind of island) for him, and began to turn the tables by betting six $ 75,000 hands at a time, for a total of $ 450,000 per hand played. In two hours, he won an unbelievable $ 26 million. It seems that Packer actually did continue to win over the following few days (that's called a *hot streak*, in this case a really phenomenal one), enough to persuade Kirk Kerkorian, the majority shareholder of the MGM group, to intervene: the management of the casino was fired on the spot – in truth, it's not clear at all why they would have been to blame – and Packer was invited to turn elsewhere for subsequent gaming sessions.

The damage was simply too great to tolerate for a man (Kerkorian) who needed – for his corporate raids – solid and stable financial foundations to support his bank loan requests. Afterwards, Packer became a Hilton customer. One staggering $ 825,000 overall bet is set in Strip history: eleven blackjack hands of $ 75,000 each... all won!

To the benefit of Steve Wynn, there was also a Packer session at the Bellagio in July 2001, where – playing baccarat this time – it seems he left $ 20 million.

For gamblers like Packer – nowadays coming mostly from China, the Middle East, Mexico and Brazil – the Vegas resorts have created the most spectacular suites in the world, including the Verona Sky Villa of the Westgate, considered the biggest hotel suite in North America (and perhaps the world). This gigantic 15,400-square-foot apartment, equipped with every possible and imaginable luxury, including a private butler, is one of three mega-suites that the Las Vegas Hilton had erected *ex novo* at the top of the original building in the mid-1990s by adding a penthouse floor and transforming the roof of the resort into the private garden of these extraordinary dwellings, in order to attract the legendary "whales".

Using Google Maps, in the satellite view you can easily identify the three private pools of the three "villa suites" of the Westgate, right at the top of the building. In addition to the Verona Sky Villa, which is the largest, there are also the Tuscany Sky Villa of 13,200 sq. ft. and the Versailles Sky Villa of 12,600 sq. ft. The latter, before the new property changed its name, was named Conrad Sky Villa, from the name of the founding patriarch of the Hilton Hotels, Conrad Hilton.

15

BILL BENNETT AND THE STRIP
FOR FAMILIES

Perhaps you will remember that Jay Sarno, the brilliant father of the Caesars Palace, had built the Circus Circus a few years later. As we have seen, the Circus Circus – conceived as a casino without hotel rooms for an adult audience – never took off and always had financial problems. In 1974, as a result of other issues due to the presence of Tony Spilotro among business owners inside the casino, Sarno and his associates – Mallin and Jacobson – did sell the property to William 'Bill' Bennett and William N. Pennington.

Of the two, Bill Bennett was the creative mind. It was Bennett, therefore, who imagined a different Strip: a Strip where even children could find hospitality, allowing daddies and mommies eager for action at the tables to take the whole family to a Las Vegas vacation. The Circus Circus became what its exterior appearance had always implied: a family resort. We shall see how this seminal idea would start a completely new phase in Strip history, which would reach its culmination in the 1990s (with the various Excalibur, Treasure Island, Luxor, MGM Grand), to close very rapidly by the end of the millennium, when the next stage of the Strip would begin with the construction of new mega-resorts dedicated mostly to adults (Bellagio, Venetian, Paris, Mandalay Bay). With the opening of the Bellagio, for the first time a Las Vegas casino hotel would expressly forbid the presence of children who were not accommodated at the Bellagio hotel itself. One of many ideas of that Strip titan named Steve Wynn, whom we'll get to know better in the next chapter.

Taking over the Circus Circus, in May 1974, cost the two partners and close friends $ 25 million ($ 125 million 2017), of which only one million came from their own pockets. The rest of the necessary funds was provided by banker E. Parry Thomas, head of the Valley Bank of Nevada, a crafty old fox who was convinced that the two partners would never be able to put back on track a casino by then on its last legs and who had funded the enterprise for the sole purpose of getting hold of the company Pennington had been forced to put at risk as collateral: Western Equities, a successful manufacturer of slot machines.

Admittedly, Thomas's reasoning seemed to make sense: the Circus Circus was hemorrhaging half a million dollars a month at the time and nobody in the city would have waged a penny on these newcomers, completely lacking management experience in the casino industry. But, you guessed it, Bennett and Pennington turned out to be way tougher cookies than expected.

Before taking control of the Circus Circus, Bennett had been studying the casino for months, touring it over and over, talking to customers and watching the employees. And he couldn't wait getting to work. And to work he got, without delay. Being persuaded that most of the resort's losses were caused by thievery and staff negligence, as well as executives' incompetence (two things that are always closely related in a casino), he proceeded to lay off the entire management of the casino, replacing it with a new group of people assembled earlier by Angel Naves, a very experienced casino manager to whom Bennett and Pennington had granted not only their trust, but also 10% of the shares of the resort.

Consider that one of the supervisors brought in by Naves, Michael Ensign, had started his career hauling coins to feed slot machines; one day, he would be COO (Chief Operating Officer) of the corporation called Circus Circus Enterprises. Another one, Antonio 'Tony' Alamo, a Cuban refugee, had begun literally from the bottom: he was a janitor. Ensign was installed as a shift manager for the most important time of the day – from the early evening hours until a couple hours after midnight – while Alamo was his deputy. Two resounding examples of meritocracy and American Dream perfectly accomplished.

According to Bennett's own estimates, in the first month of operation alone the new management did save $ 100,000 (half a million dollars 2017) thanks to the clampdown on theft and other misdeeds by casino staff. Spilotro was forever removed from the Strip, though he didn't go empty-handed: Bennett and Pennington were forced to buy back his license for the gift shop located on Circus Circus premises, at a price well above its real value.

The next step needed to revamp the property was to recreate an environment more conducive to gambling: Bennett got rid of bears, elephants and similar nonsense, moving clowns and trapeze artists upstairs – we are still talking about a resort called Circus, after all – and away from the players. Pennington, meanwhile, had settled for a secondary role, working during the week in Reno, Nevada – where he continued to run his Western Equities company – and flying every weekend to Vegas to keep himself updated on developments.

Another innovation, which would prove to be very useful for Circus Circus's financial health and would help – many years later – to inspire the family-friendly period of the Strip, was the creation of a kind of indoor amusement park where parents could leave their kids lightheartedly, to go squander the family assets at slot machines and table games. But the decisive change of course, destined to save the resort and allowing it to become the heart of a rising casino empire, was the idea – entirely Bennett's – to completely change the customer base of the casino.

Until then, all Strip resorts had always tried to

attract more or less affluent customers, able to leave thousands of dollars at the gaming tables without blinking an eye. Bennett, however, did realize that it was time for Las Vegas to lose its aura of exclusivity and to become accessible to a completely uncharted clientele: the humble working class, laborers and truckers among them. On average, they would spend (and lose) much less than the old customers, of course, but there were many more of them. This idea seemed almost heretical in the eyes of other resort owners on the Strip, but Bennett was no fool: he had observed and studied the explosion of the McDonald's phenomenon since the 1960s and he had learned some useful lessons. His motto became: «To provide customers with all the excitement of the Strip without the prices of the Strip.»

In line with this innovative business model, Bennett increased the number of slot machines – traditionally considered useful only to keep players' wives and girlfriends busy while the gentlemen were gambling serious money at blackjack and craps – up to occupying 70% of the entire casino floor, about double as much as usual at the time. We can say that promotion to the most important source of profit for any casino, which slot machines would keep for decades, took place thanks to this Bill Bennett intuition.

In 1975, Bennett built a second 15-story tower with 395 hotel rooms, bringing the total to 795. Today the Circus Circus has over 3,700 rooms in all, including motel-style lodging.

The two resorts created by Bennett from scratch on the Strip, the Excalibur and the Luxor, play a role of such importance in the recent history of the city to be deserving of two dedicated chapters later. We will now proceed in a rigorous chronological order in presenting the following casino hotels to have risen along the Strip since 1989.

16

STEVE WYNN AND THE MIRAGE

You are about to read one of the most extraordinary, exciting and interesting chapters in this story. It could not be any different, in my opinion, since I'm going to introduce to you a man whose name has become synonymous with Las Vegas for so many reasons and whose illuminated signature stands out in the sky at the north end of the Strip: I'm talking, it's almost pleonastic to say it, about the only, inimitable, unequaled Steve Wynn, born Stephen Alan Weinberg.

Jay Sarno had imagined the first example of entertainment architecture, creating that splendid palace of excess called Caesars Palace and changing the face of the Strip forever. Howard Hughes had been instrumental in expelling the last emissaries of the Italian and Jewish Mafia out of Vegas and in paving the way for the big corporations, who would raise the bar of what could be done to previously inconceivable heights. Kirk Kerkorian, following in the footsteps of the first two, would be able to inaugurate the world's largest hotel thrice (the International – now Westgate – in 1969; the MGM Grand – now Bally's – in 1973; again the MGM Grand – the current one – in 1993).

Steve Wynn, with the Mirage, would help the Strip

step it up a notch once again. And this – in my opinion – is one of the most unique and fascinating features of the city we are celebrating: the ability to reinvent itself unceasingly and never lack the ambition to evolve and improve what already seemed to be the pinnacle.

The construction of the Mirage, Wynn's first project in Las Vegas, would be a milestone in Strip history for two reasons. For starters, it was the first and only casino hotel built along the Strip in the 1980s and it did put an end to a really difficult time for the city, marked by a long economic stagnation and the arrival on the scene of a fearsome competitor, destined to affect the customer base coming from the North East: Atlantic City, where gambling was legalized in 1976. Additionally, it was the first resort funded by the issue of junk bonds, the notorious "high risk and high performance" securities whose main expert was Michael Milken at investment bank Drexel Burnham Lambert, who later inevitably became great friends with Wynn.

With Milken's help, Wynn managed to raise the jaw-dropping sum of $ 630 million (equivalent to $ 1.25 billion today) and to realize the resort of his dreams, so spectacular – in his intentions – to make instantly obsolete every casino hotel to be found at the time along the Strip. Well... goal fully achieved!

Before presenting the Mirage and all its wonders, it's worth telling a little about the adventurous life of

Steve Wynn in the years before 1989. Steve's dad – Michael Weinberg – was allowed to change his last name in 1946, in order to prevent the risk of anti-Semitic discrimination. Steve grew up in Utica, a small town in the state of New York. Michael Wynn (formerly Weinberg) owned some bingo parlors in several states on the East Coast. His attempt to expand into Las Vegas was unsuccessful: his application for a gambling license was rejected, most likely because Wynn lacked the right contacts, or *juice* in Vegas parlance (it's 1952).

Steve's parents did want him to be a lawyer and they sent him to study law at the University of Pennsylvania, in Philadelphia. During a family vacation in Florida, where the Wynns stayed at the legendary Fontainebleau Hotel in Miami Beach – considered the most significant project by famous architect Morris Lapidus –, Steve met Elaine Pascal, the daughter of a friend of his father, and the two started dating.

In 1963, Steve's life changed radically. His father Mike died during an open-heart surgery, a very rare and risky procedure at the time, and Steve – at age 21 – suddenly became his family's breadwinner, with responsibility for the welfare of his mother and his younger brother and a bingo parlor to run in Maryland (the activity had downsized to one room only).

In June 1967, finally, Wynn moved to Las Vegas with the whole family. Including Elaine, who had become – in the meantime – his wife. With the help of banker E. Parry Thomas, chairman of the Valley Bank (already met in the previous chapter), in 1972 Wynn succeeded in mastering a coup, which provided him with the financial clout necessary to lay the foundations of his empire. Wynn did buy from Howard Hughes a small plot adjacent to the Caesars Palace, which Hughes was renting to that casino as a parking area. The necessary money, of course, came from Thomas.

Clifford Perlman, Caesars Palace's president, was not happy at all and tried to immediately buy back the land from Wynn. But Wynn had a more ambitious project: he told Perlman that if Caesars did not agree to pay him a stratospheric amount, he would build on that short stretch overlooking the Strip a small casino – a parasite casino, in industry jargon – that, one step away from Caesars' entrance, would risk to attract a part of the clientele directed to the casino of the Strip behemoth. Perlman, aware of the support Wynn enjoyed from Thomas, was forced to surrender.

Thanks to this deal, Wynn made a net profit of $ 800,000 (equivalent to $ 4,750,000 today), sufficient to provide a solid foundation for his subsequent undertakings. The *Las Vegas Sun* wrote in those days: «At the age of 30, Steve Wynn concluded a deal many men much more experienced than him would give an eye for», adding that Wynn was «rapidly rising to fame and power.» A spot-on prediction, no doubt about it!

With this success under his belt, with Thomas having his back and the Valley Bank funds at his disposal, Wynn prepared himself to make a definitive leap forward, which would sanction his role as a key player in Las Vegas history that he would not abandon to this day. He decided to target the Golden Nugget, a historic downtown casino that found itself in dire straits (see chapter 7). In 1973, Wynn managed to become a major shareholder of the GN and to take over the reins. At just 31, he was the youngest casino owner in Nevada history. Having very clear ideas about what he wanted the Golden Nugget to be, he began a thorough renovation and – for the first time – made a posh place of it. The GN lounge became a really cool venue, also thanks to entertainers of great renown that Steve did not hesitate to sign: Frank Sinatra, Diana Ross and Kenny Rogers among them.

In the first year of the new ownership, Golden Nugget's pretax profit quintupled, reaching $ 4,200,000 (about $ 21 million today). To help him relaunch the property and to position it differently from the downtown-area casino hotels, typically considered as squalid, Wynn devised a TV commercial where Frank Sinatra in the flesh warned Wynn to leave enough towels in his room and even gave him a tip. Simply priceless!

In July 1979, Wynn laid the foundation stone of the Golden Nugget Atlantic City. Having witnessed the enormous success that the first casinos inaugurated on the Boardwalk (the popular Atlantic City waterfront promenade) were achieving – with never-before-seen profits in the gaming industry –, Wynn did not want to stand by and watch. The new casino hotel, inaugurated on December 9, 1980, with 500 rooms, did cost a whopping $ 160 million ($ 480 million today), but made a $ 18 million profit in the first six months of operation, as much as the other seven casinos open at that time in Atlantic City put together: a true record.

But back to Las Vegas: in 1986, Wynn was ready at last to become one of the great Strip characters, in the same league as the ones we've met so far. That year, he sold the Golden Nugget on the Boardwalk to Bally Manufacturing Corp., which was also taking over the first MGM Grand in Vegas from Kirk Kerkorian, and he cashed $ 440 million for it (about $ 1 billion today). It is estimated that his personal fortune at that time amounted to $ 75 million (about $ 170 million today), a figure more than enough to allow him to devote himself to even more ambitious projects. And ambition is a personality trait Steve never really lacked!

On November 22, 1989, the Mirage opened its doors on the Strip and turned out to be an immediate hit. It was the birth of a new breed of resorts, sometimes called *super casino*, and had cost – as we have seen – $ 630 million at the time. Part of the cost was due to the gold dust (real gold) needed to give the desired coloring to the windows. The building layout was the one that would become a classic of the Strip, i.e. that triform structure inaugurated by architect Martin Stern with Kirk Kerkorian's International in 1969. The three buildings were – and still are – of identical dimensions, for a total of 3,000 rooms.

Within a few months, the Mirage became the most visited tourist site in the entire State of Nevada, beating even the Hoover Dam. It should surprise only to a certain extent, considering the opulence of the common spaces, the small tropical forest housed in the atrium (flooded with natural light coming from above: something never seen before in Vegas), the number and quality of restaurants – there are 14 in all today, including a Starbucks – and, above all, the fake volcano that "erupts" at regular intervals from sunset until late at night. Wynn had brought the concept of entertainment architecture to the extreme. Now the show moved from the inside of the resort to the outside, visible to all passers-by. The spectacular and immense swimming pool immersed in greenery and equipped with a large waterfall also deserves a mention.

As if that were not enough, Wynn also revolutionized the concept of evening show: he hired the German magicians and tamers – American naturalized citizens – Siegfried Fischbacher and Roy Horn (a couple in life too), who brought to Las Vegas a spectacle of magic and big cats, including the famous white tigers. The duo, simply called Siegfried & Roy, would perform at the Mirage uninterruptedly from 1990 until October 3, 2003, when the unthinkable happened: Roy Horn was attacked suddenly and unpredictably by one of his beloved white tigers during a show. Horn did suffer life-threatening injuries, including serious neck injuries, and had at least one heart attack. A quarter of his skull was removed to relieve the pressure of a brain hematoma. Incredibly, Roy Horn not only did survive, but is today able to talk and walk again, albeit with difficulty. Following Horn's explicit desire, not a finger was laid on that tiger. As a side note, it is believed Horn was in the process of suffering a heart attack *before* his tiger mauled him, and that the animal was in fact trying to *save* him, not to kill him.

That's the story of Steve Wynn's ascent in the Las Vegas firmament – we'll meet him again later – and of the birth of the Mirage, which represented a real turning point for the city. So much so that a reporter wrote: «Steve Wynn's face is now the face of Las Vegas.» Before meeting the last of the great Strip personalities I intend to present, we shall briefly introduce the casino hotels opened in sequence after the Mirage: the Excalibur, the Luxor, the Treasure Island and the MGM Grand.

17

MR. SHERWIN, LUCKY DEVIL

With regard to the Mirage inauguration, let me tell you a story that's quite extraordinary. Warning: Reading not recommended to those who suffer from envy attacks!

A few hours after the inauguration of the brand-new and spectacular Mirage, a man named Elmer Sherwin won the jackpot at a slot machine connected to the Megabucks network. Megabucks slots' purpose is to create a giant progressive jackpot, which grows second by second (you can follow its development directly above the machine itself) by taking advantage of a tiny withdrawal from hundreds of slot machines scattered across many different casinos. Megabucks machines are an exclusive of IGT (International Game Technology Plc), a company with offices in Las Vegas and Reno and listed on the New York Stock Exchange. The goal is to reach very tempting jackpots, in the millions of dollars, enough to raise the interest of the public and the media.

Well, this Elmer Sherwin, a Las Vegas resident, brought home a check worth $ 4,662,177, over $ 9 million in 2017. It was the highest winnings ever obtained through a slot machine in Nevada. Obviously, this almost instant hit was also a great coup for the Mirage itself, which enjoyed a fair amount of free advertising. But, to this point, we are still in the realm of the possible. It was sixteen years later that Sherwin became a living legend. On September 15, 2005, Mr. Sherwin – by then 92 – again won the Megabucks jackpot, this time playing a Cannery Casino slot, a casino with a small hotel (200 rooms) located a few miles north of downtown. This time, the jackpot amounted to $ 21,147,947 (nearly $ 27 million in 2017 dollars). IGT was unable to calculate the mathematical probability of such an event... twice!

18

EXCALIBUR (1990 – still open)

Steve Wynn was not alone in imagining a different future for the Strip in the second half of the 1980s.

At the time, the most thriving gaming company in the world was Circus Circus Enterprises, the creature of Bill Bennett and Bill Pennington. In 1983, with the help of Michael Milken (who had already provided the financial propellant for the realization of Wynn's projects), Bennett had listed the company on the New York Stock Exchange, thus obtaining easier access to the capital needed to expand his empire, in addition to a substantial increase in the personal wealth of the two main partners. In those years, the three properties of Circus Circus Enterprises, the Circus Circus on the Strip and another in Reno, plus a third casino hotel in Laughlin, Nevada, boasted an unbelievable 99% average room occupancy and an enviable financial health. In 1986, Bennett and Pennington entered the Forbes 400 list of wealthiest Americans for the first time. The personal assets of both friends were estimated at $ 250 million each ($ 560 million today). On this basis, the company planned a much more ambitious future.

When Wynn announced in 1987 that he would

build a new resort of a level never before seen on the Strip (that would become the Mirage), Bennett hastened to make an announcement: also Circus Circus Ent. would build its new crown jewel. Only, it would have 4,000 rooms instead of the 3,000 of the Mirage, and would be the largest hotel in the world. Faithful to the principle of the Strip accessible to everyone, Bennett ordered to design a family-friendly resort, much less luxurious than the Mirage, but – at the same time – more welcoming for families with children and for less well-off strata of the population. The idea for the Excalibur was born.

On June 19, 1990, the Excalibur opened its doors. The layout was definitely innovative: four identical 28-story buildings – of 1,000 rooms each – positioned to form a quadrilateral, almost like an ancient fortress. In fact, the architecture was clearly inspired by some medieval castles, but revisited in fairytale-style. The total cost of the resort was "only" $ 300 million ($ 570 million today), less than half the Mirage, which proves the completely different level of luxury and detail of the two resorts and the different customer base they were aimed to. Even today, the Excalibur hosts the only show genuinely dedicated to kids of the whole Strip: Tournament of Kings, complete with horses (real ones) and knights (fake ones).

As anticipated, it was at the time the largest hotel in the world, a record it would lose three years later in favor of the current MGM Grand (with 5,000 rooms).

The Excalibur immediately was a huge success, so much so that it made a pretax profit of $ 80 million during its first year of operation, or 26.6% of construction costs. The 1990s boom was underway.

19

LUXOR (1993 – still open)

As we have seen, in those years two key players were at the root of the rebirth of the Strip, which was quickly coming out of a phase not at all rosy: Steve Wynn and Bill Bennett.

Bennett had inaugurated the Excalibur only seven months after the inauguration of Steve Wynn's Mirage. But he didn't really like the role of runner-up. When Wynn announced in the fall of 1991 that he would build a second resort right next to the Mirage – to be inaugurated by the end of 1993 – Bennett did not hesitate one second and announced that Circus Circus Enterprises would build a mega-resort that would be revolutionary in its architecture: a 2,500-room glass pyramid. The project was simply called Project X, because the final name had not been chosen yet. This time, however, Bennett was determined to win the race against Wynn: the Luxor (this was the name chosen for the new resort) would open before the Treasure Island (the new Wynn resort), come what may. All the more because Kirk Kerkorian, one of the Strip greats, was getting back in the game: his company would build the new MGM Grand – exactly twenty years after the birth of the first – which would be (do I need to say it?) the largest hotel in the world. Right in the face of Bennett's Excalibur.

At the time, Circus Circus Ent. was so rich in cash that it could afford to finance the new venture without the help of bank loans or bond issues: a really exceptional event, that wouldn't be repeated in Strip history. Bennett won the race he cared so much about: the Luxor was inaugurated on October 15, 1993, twelve days before the Treasure Island.

A 30-story black pyramid hence stood out against the sky in the Nevada desert, almost like in Luxor, Egypt! At that time, with its height of 110 meters, it was the tallest building on the Strip. To tell the truth, the project initially had the pyramid covered with gold-colored glass surfaces, such as those used by Wynn for the Mirage. Because of the exorbitant cost of those (as already explained, you need authentic gold dust to get the desired effect), Bennet made do with much cheaper brown glass. In retrospect, it was probably a lucky decision: the black pyramid is magnificent, as well as unique, and its shades change several times over the course of the day, depending on the position of the sun. For years, before the LED lighting on the four edges was installed, the Luxor would disappear completely in the dark of the night, with the exception of the powerful light beam at the top of the pyramid.

The final cost was $ 375 million ($ 640 million today), 20% over budget. Once inaugurated, problems for the resort began to pile up from the first day. For starters, right at the end of the construction work a further $ 25 million would have been necessary to achieve perfection, but Bennett – obsessed with his race with Wynn – wouldn't listen to reason and refused to make available the funds required to complete everything that would be needed in order to guarantee a smooth start.

Wynn, with a real masterstroke, had announced that the Treasure Island would be inaugurated on the same day as the Luxor. At that point, Bennett, aware of how much visibility he would have lost had it happened, pushed everyone to accelerate operations as much as possible, in order to earn him a couple of weeks. The result was indeed achieved, but at a high price. The resort did open without really being completed, much less brought up to speed.

The Luxor is in fact an immense covered atrium (certainly the largest in the world at the time; am not sure about today) with the rooms arranged along the pyramid facades and the room doors aligned along the balconies overlooking the atrium. When dozens of water pipes exploded during the early days of activity, because incorrectly installed and never tested, veritable waterfalls formed and began to fall from above on visitors and guests. Imagine: twenty-five-story waterfalls inside an enormous hotel. A spectacle not to be missed! Most of the more than 2,500 rooms were not even ready. One guest complained of having been sent to a room with five TV sets but no bed!

To save money, Bennett had not installed service elevators. Therefore, customers and service personnel (with food trolleys, dirty linens, etc.) were forced to use the same elevators – called "inclinators", rather than elevators, because they climbed obliquely along the four edges of the pyramid – with the consequences you can imagine. As if that were not enough, the tram installed to connect the two neighboring properties of Circus Circus (Excalibur and Luxor), called monorail, was out of order almost immediately. Instead of having it repaired at once and litigating later, Bennett decided to sue the builder and claim damages, and in the meantime the tram was lying idle.

The last mistake had been to snub taxi drivers and travel agents, for which no traditional evening show preview was organized – the show was called *Winds of the Gods* –, so that no one was willing to recommend a Luxor evening show to tourists who visited the city. The Luxor, built by Bennett at the height of his career and power, would become his gravestone, professionally speaking. Within a year, Bennett would be dismissed from the corporation he had made big and respected. Who knows if he has had the wit to appreciate the irony of the whole affair, since a pyramid – after all – is effectively a tomb.

In 1998, to the north of the original pyramid, two rather anonymous black glass towers were added, bringing the total number of rooms to 4,400. Between 2008 and 2009, following extensive renovation work on interior spaces, the openly *faux Egypt* theme of the common spaces and rooms was almost completely lost, in keeping with the new style of interior design that now dominates the Strip, which we could define "neutral luxury". In the next chapter, I'll tell the story of the casino hotel whose shadow alone was enough to put an end to Bennett's career: Steve Wynn's Treasure Island.

20

TREASURE ISLAND (1993 – still open)

We have seen in the previous chapter how the Treasure Island was the indirect cause of the demise of Bill Bennett, a great protagonist of the 1970s and 1980s. It's time to tell the salient facts about this fascinating resort.

At the end of the race between Wynn and Bennett on who would first open their new casino hotel, the Treasure Island was inaugurated on October 27, 1993, with 32 floors and nearly 2,900 rooms. It cost $ 450 million (about $ 770 million today). The race with the Luxor – much further south on the Strip – was lost, but the Treasure Island won by far the only race that counts: the one about success and revenues. After all, the preconditions were great. Wynn, as always, had done an excellent job, both architecturally – so much so that even today the hotel is one of the most original and aesthetically pleasing of the Strip – and from the point of view of the substance.

As for the exterior, Wynn had devised a battle between a British crown ship (the Britannia) and one of pirates (the Hispaniola) that took place several times every night in a small artificial lake located between the hotel and the Strip, complete with a lot of cannon shots (fake) and a ship boarding (real). Needless to say, being this Las Vegas, pirates invariably came out victorious! Inside, the banner was held high by the first major production in Las Vegas of the much celebrated Cirque du Soleil (Circus of the Sun), the company founded in 1984 by Canadians Guy Laliberté and Gilles S.te-Croix that had invented and developed the concept of a circus show with no animals involved.

At the time, Cirque du Soleil was a small organization with a single traveling show, *Saltimbanco*. Wynn already knew this group, having hosted their show (*Nouvelle Expérience*) at the Mirage for a year and, having been impressed, decided to make it the main show of his new resort. On Christmas Eve 1993, *Mystère* debuted at the Treasure Island – where it still performs today – and we can say that that was the decisive turning point for a circus company that would become legendary. Suffice it to say that, over the years, *Mystère* has been crowned best show in town by *Las Vegas Review Journal* readers nine times.

Today, Cirque du Soleil has 5,000 employees (including acrobats, gymnasts, swimmers, musicians, etc.), twenty shows between itinerant and resident – seven of which on the Strip – and revenues of over 800 million dollars annually. Many of the gymnasts and swimmers are former professional athletes, sometimes Olympians, who are hired when their competitive career is about to end. I think the safest advice one can give to Vegas visitors is not to leave the city without watching at least one of Cirque's shows, which are beyond anything you can expect from an evening show. The spectrum of choices, as we have seen, is wide. Ticket prices, unfortunately, are no peanuts either.

Let's recall, at this point, a little-known episode in Steve Wynn's life, that happened just before the opening of the Treasure Island. On July 26, 1993, Wynn's eldest daughter, Kevyn (twenty-seven years of age at the time), was kidnapped by a gang of thugs while returning home. Wynn, contacted by phone, took the matter in his own hands and, without even notifying the police, negotiated a ransom of $ 1.45 million ($ 2.5 million today), which he handed over personally following the kidnappers' instructions. The kidnapping, luckily, lasted two and a half hours in all and ended without any damage to Kevyn. Once informed, the police got to work with special zeal – don't forget we are in Nevada, where the salary of government officials of all kinds is effectively paid for by taxes on casinos' earnings – and, in 72 hours, it identified the gang leader, mostly thanks to phone records. The scoundrel was arrested in California on August 1, six days after the kidnapping, while trying to buy a Ferrari paying cash. An true genius! A few days later, his two accomplices were also arrested.

In 2000, shortly after the completion of the

Bellagio (inaugurated on October 15, 1998), Kirk Kerkorian, the phenomenally wealthy and never-satisfied tycoon, managed to put his hands on the company of which Wynn was the majority shareholder, Mirage Resorts Incorporated, as a result of a hostile takeover. To complete the acquisition, MGM Grand Inc. had to spend $ 6.6 billion ($ 9.5 billion today), thus becoming MGM Mirage. Wynn, who wasn't even thinking about retiring to private life, had meanwhile bought the venerable Desert Inn, which was still a classy place but had been in decline for some time, for $ 270 million ($ 385 million today), and was preparing to start again from scratch – so to speak – designing what will become the Wynn Las Vegas (plus the Encore a little later).

The last chapter in the story of the Treasure Island was written in March 2009, when the resort was sold to entrepreneur Phil Ruffin, active in the oil and real estate businesses as well as in the casino industry, currently #315 of the *Forbes 400* ranking of the wealthiest Americans, with a personal fortune estimated at $ 2.7 billion. He would rename the property T.I. (though everybody still uses the old name) and would transform the historic battle between regular navy and pirates into a rather spicy show unsuitable for an underage audience: *Sirens of TI*, where a group of scantily dressed "sirens" challenges the poor pirates, who were accustomed to entirely different battles. One thing is certain: the short-lived family-friendly period of Vegas – which has reached its peak with the resorts Circus Circus, Excalibur, Luxor, Treasure Island and MGM Grand too, as we shall see – is officially over. Just as the open-air show of the Treasure Island, definitively closed by Ruffin on October 20, 2013.

As an aside, let's mention that on January 6, 2008, Phil Ruffin did marry – at the age of 72 – the then 26-year-old model Oleksandra Nikolayenko, Miss Ukraine 2004.

This is the story of an often underestimated casino hotel, which perhaps was deserving of a more prominent place in the history of the city.

21

MGM GRAND (1993 – still open)

On December 18, 1993, at the intersection with Tropicana Avenue, the majestic MGM Grand was inaugurated. Kirk Kerkorian had done it again: for the third time in 24 years, he had conceived and built the world's largest hotel, taking back the title from the Excalibur, right across the street. Its price tag was $ 1.1 billion at the time (about $ 1.9 billion today) and it was built on the grounds of the old Tropicana Country Club. This immense resort hosts no less than 5,000 rooms (5,005 officially), along with what was – at the time – the largest casino in the world, with an astounding surface of 171,000 sq. ft.

The area dedicated to the three swimming pools measured a whopping 140,000 sq. ft, later expanded. The valet parking area has a capacity of 1,200 cars, while 4,800 parking spaces are available in self-parking areas. The cross-like structure becomes interesting in the west-facing arm, Strip-side, where a stepped tower was created that – becoming larger at the base – allows the creation of suites with an outdoor terrace, from which guests can enjoy a spectacular view of the other Strip resorts, especially at night, and the pleasant desert evening breeze.

Not too many people are aware of a peculiar fact concerning the MGM Grand: right at the extremity of the west tower – the stepped one – was a small hotel by the standards of modern Strip resorts (it had 714 rooms), which was simply incorporated in the immense structure of the new casino hotel. Why this hotel, called the Marina (even the name made little sense, in the middle of the desert), escaped its most natural destiny – to be imploded to make room for the new Strip colossus – remains a mystery.

Talking about the MGM Grand, it's impossible not to mention the lion, always the emblem of the company: just think about the countless movies we've seen at the cinema or on television with the roaring lion before the opening credits. At the inauguration, a gigantic lion head placed right at the corner of the Strip and Tropicana Avenue served as the entrance to the resort. In practice, to gain access to the casino customers needed to go through a passage placed under the lion's mouth and between its front paws. In 1997, this characteristic symbol of the property was replaced by a more traditional bronze statue depicting a seated lion, considered to be the largest bronze sculpture in North America and the second biggest world-wide, with a height of 70 feet including the pedestal and a weight of 50 tons. It seems that Chinese gamblers, known to be among the most superstitious in the world and whose importance for the Las Vegas economy was beginning to grow exponentially at that time, refused to pass "through" the mouth of the feline, an act capable of drawing bad luck on the players, apparently.

The huge Grand Garden Arena, with a maximum capacity of 16,800 seats (depending on the event), was inaugurated with a glorious New Year's Eve performance by Barbra Streisand on December 31, 1993. Over the years, this facility would host both concerts of the most in-demand bands and numerous sports events, including the most important boxing matches. It was here that Mike Tyson, on June 28, 1997, did detach half an ear of Evander Holyfield biting him during an infamous World Heavyweight Championship.

The historical interest of this resort – which is still today in a state-of-the-art condition, having recently undergone extensive renovation and redevelopment of the hotel rooms – also lies in its gigantic amusement park, inspired by the attractions of the first Disneyland (located in Anaheim, California) and of Universal Studios in Hollywood. Called MGM Grand Adventures and costing 10% of the total investment for the resort, it covered an area of 33 acres. This theme park was the last and most massive attempt to make the Strip a family-friendly destination where children could feel welcome. Its closure after less than seven years of activity in 2000 would mark the end of this idea, initially explored – as you may recall – by Bill Bennett, first with the renewed Circus Circus and then with the

Excalibur.

As usual, the first man to understand that the tide was turning had been Steve Wynn, who had previously tried this route with the Treasure Island, albeit not too forcefully. On October 15, 1998, he had inaugurated the Bellagio, the first Strip resort specifically targeted to adults only, with no access to children who were not staying at the hotel, a spectacular botanical garden and – surprise, surprise – a remarkably well-stocked art gallery (that originally hosted Wynn's private art collection). At present, the Strip counts just one amusement park, indoor and much more modest: the Adventuredome at the Circus Circus. Visitors over 21 years of age, the only ones allowed to drink alcohol and gamble, have successfully reclaimed the city!

The space once occupied by the deceased Grand Adventures park was used to expand the pool area, to build a more profitable conference center and to erect the three white towers called The Signature at MGM Grand, inaugurated in 2006-2007. The project called for six of them, to be sold to customers interested in investing in the city taking advantage of the condo-hotel model, i.e. studios and one- or two-bedroom apartments to be used freely for their personal needs and to rent out to paying guests the rest of the year, such as normal hotel rooms. The collapse of the real estate market in 2007, followed by the well-known and quite long-term Great Recession, resulted in a downsizing of the project to three towers, containing

576 units each. Being equipped with a large refrigerator and a fully stocked kitchen, they are an excellent solution for longer stays in the city and for anyone not willing to be tied to restaurants and buffets for three meals a day.

To my knowledge, the value-for-money of these rooms and suites is generally considered to be very good and The Signature is especially appreciated by visitors who prefer to take a break from the Strip madness for at least a few hours a day, thanks to the absence of a casino inside the towers, to the dedicated entrance and to the private swimming pools.

I could not close the description of this resort – which is home to the impressive number of 19 different restaurants – without mentioning The Mansion at MGM Grand. It is an entire area, located immediately north of the old Marina, occupied by a sort of mega-villa in Tuscan style, which houses – by all accounts – the most luxurious accommodations available on the Strip. This building – a genuine oasis of peace – has 29 absolutely exclusive suites, equipped with every comfort, ranging from 2,400 sq. ft. of the most "modest" one to over 12,000 sq. ft. of the most over-the-top one. It goes without saying that only the most important guests of the casino, meaning the players who love to bet outrageously high amounts of money at the gaming tables, have access to this corner of the resort, obviously "free of charge". A small army of 140 people – including multilingual butlers, waiters, gardeners, chefs, etc. – is dedicated exclusively to making a stay at The Mansion unforgettable and to satisfy every whim of the lucky guests staying there.

So concludes the chapter dedicated to the iconic MGM Grand. It has never been the tallest hotel on the Strip, but it still is – twenty-five years later – the largest.

22

SHELDON ADELSON AND
THE VENETIAN

Sheldon Gary Adelson represents the perfect nemesis of Steve Wynn in Las Vegas: both Jews, both committed conservatives and Republicans (Adelson is one of the main financial backers of Republican presidential campaigns, while Wynn has always been openly critical of President Obama's policies), both very skilled businessmen (we already learned about Wynn's ascent; now we'll meet Adelson) and both endowed with a dominant personality, scarcely inclined to compromise, these great protagonists of recent Vegas history never missed a chance to challenge each other.

Adelson, who celebrated his 85th birthday in August 2017, is the classic self-made man. Born in a family of modest means (his father was a taxi driver while his mother was a seamstress), he had to start working soon: at 12 years of age he was already delivering newspapers in his Boston neighborhood, while at the same time holding out against bullying by his Irish peers. He would then work in the financial sector and briefly attend college in New York, without ever graduating.

Adelson's career as a multi-billionaire began with the creation of COMDEX (Computer Dealers' Exhibition) with a group of business partners, a specialized IT exhibition that would become the benchmark for the entire industry. Beginning in 1979, every year in November thousands of exhibitors and over 100,000 visitors would return to Las Vegas to attend this trade show, with a remarkable 200,000 visitors record in the 2000 edition. The downturn came quickly: the 2003 edition saw only 500 exhibitors and 40,000 visitors and was the last one for this exhibition that had become a symbol of the city. The CES (Consumer Electronics Show) now rules in its place, with numbers similar to COMDEX's most successful years.

Adelson and his associates had in the meantime withdrawn from the company: in 1995 they had sold the company owning Comdex to the Japanese SoftBank Corporation for $ 862 million, of which $ 500 million ($ 810 million today) were Adelson's share. Following that deal, the ambitious and enterprising Adelson would not stop again, rapidly climbing positions in the Olympus of Sin City and of super-rich Americans.

Way back in 1988, Adelson and his partners had bought the legendary Sands, then already obsolete, only to tear it down towards the end of 1996. In the spring of 1997, Adelson announced that he would build, in the area previously occupied by the Sands, the largest resort in the world, that would be inspired by the city of Venice (Italy): as we know, Americans are crazy about Italian art cities. It would have been a pretty perfect replica of some of the most famous Venetian vistas – such as the Doge Palace, the Rialto Bridge and the San Marco Bell Tower – complete with copies of famous frescoes in the casino area.

The initial project included 6,000 rooms, or – more precisely – 6,000 suites, since Adelson had decided to create something unique: the hotel with the largest rooms ever seen on the Strip. The standard room, in fact, measures 650 sq. ft. (including a vast bathroom) and is divided into a sleeping area and a living area, a kind of sitting room next to the window. Later on, the project was reduced to a less ambitious 3,000 rooms, but the final cost did nonetheless reach the considerable $ 1.5 billion mark ($ 2.2 billion today), placing it second in the world, just behind Steve Wynn's Bellagio (who else?), inaugurated on October 15, 1998 at a cost of $ 1.6 billion ($ 2.4 billion today). Sophia Loren – as a guarantor of Italianness – and Cher – as a performer – attended the inauguration of The Venetian Las Vegas (its full name) on May 3, 1999. A second tower, adjacent to the first one and called the Venezia Tower, would be added in 2003, bringing the total number of rooms to just over 4,000.

In an attempt to recreate a more realistic Venetian atmosphere, Adelson did not forget the famous canals with their gondolas, not to mention the "gondoliers", who were even charged with performing songs of dubious quality. I point out that the gondolas are not exactly the same as those in Venice, as they move along a fixed path, dragged on tracks placed on the bottom of the canals themselves.

At this point I can reveal a little secret: the Venetian was not the first resort of the Strip equipped with a "navigable" channel. The idea had previously been introduced by Bill Bennett with the Luxor, where a waterway that was intended to represent the Nile River ran along the perimeter of the atrium at the base of the pyramid. The idea was that hotel guests were to be transported on Egyptian-style boats from the check-in area to the elevators, which – as we know – are located at the four corners of the pyramid. There were even employees dressed up as Ancient Egyptians who translated the "hieroglyphs" visible in various places of the pyramid during the transfer along the... Nile. This idea was so successful that it became a real problem for the casino: imagined exclusively for hotel guests' transportation, the boats were quickly stormed by tourists who were not staying at the hotel, to the point that Luxor's management put on sale tickets to make use of this attraction.

Hard to believe, the boat trip inside the pyramid became so popular that it forced the management to raise ticket prices several times in rapid succession to try to reduce the influx of tourists. It was clear, in fact, that the time spent by customers on board these boats was time stolen to gambling in the casino. And the casino is the cash cow of every resort. In 1996 the "Nile tour" had to be closed and, where the "river" once was flowing, rows of more conventional and more profitable slot machines were installed.

It is worth mentioning that Adelson is the only owner of Strip resorts to take on with no reverential fear at all the very powerful Culinary Union, the workers' union supporting employees in the hospitality and food service industry, which – as you can easily imagine – in a city like Las Vegas is quite dominant. Adelson, faithful to his ultra-liberal principles, has always denied access to his properties to the union, incurring its wrath and even causing some retaliation attempts.

Adelson's mega-project on the Strip would be completed with the realization of his second casino hotel: the Palazzo, adjacent and connected to the Venetian, was inaugurated on December 30, 2007. In fact, that is the opening date of the casino, just in time to benefit from the most profitable days of the year, while the official inauguration of the entire resort took place on January 17, 2008. It cost $ 1.8 billion (over $ 2 billion 2017) and has just over 3,000 rooms, slightly larger and even more luxurious than Venetian's ones. With 196 meters and 53 floors, this is the third tallest building in Nevada, positioned behind the

Stratosphere Tower and the Fontainebleau (that never opened), but also holds an impressive record: it is, by internal surface, the largest single building existing in the United States, with a total floor area just shy of 7 million sq. ft.

It was during the design of this second resort that one of the most passionate clashes of tycoons that the Strip had ever seen took place: Steve Wynn, indeed, repeatedly tried to throw up roadblocks against Adelson, claiming that the project did not provide for a sufficient number of parking spaces and that already many Venetian employees were forced to park at adjacent resorts, taking away precious space intended for the casinos' clientele. The dispute dragged on for much of 2004: Wynn, who was putting the finishing touches to his new resort just north of the Venetian and the planned Palazzo (Wynn Las Vegas, to be inaugurated on April 28, 2005), wanted at all costs to resolve the issue before his valuable guests could encounter intolerable parking problems.

Only in February 2005 did the two rivals bury the hatchet, after the Clark County Commission, in charge of overseeing this kind of problems, had warned the contenders that patience was starting to wear thin as a result of ongoing complaints and counter-claims filed by attorneys working for Wynn and Adelson.

On a final note, Adelson can rightly claim to have built the world's second largest resort, though the over 7,000 hotel rooms in total are distributed within two distinct casino hotels and three separate buildings. As of today, the largest resort in the world is actually located in Asia: the First World Hotel in Pahang, Malaysia, with 7,351 rooms between two hotel towers.

We'll see in the last chapter of this book how Adelson, like Wynn, has been able to diversify into markets more promising than Vegas to preserve his role as a key player in the casino industry. Exactly what allows him to occupy today the 14th rank on the *Forbes 400* list of wealthiest Americans, with personal assets estimated at $ 35.1 billion. Much richer than his rival Wynn, whose fortune apparently amounts to one-tenth of his (plus a sizable portion that went to ex-wife Elaine).

23

THE FABULOUS 1990s

As we have seen in previous chapters, the 1970s and 1980s were not good years for the economy and the city of Las Vegas. It was the audacity of men like Steve Wynn and Bill Bennett to revitalize the legendary Strip in great style, after it had lost much of the allure it had in the 1950s and 1960s. The opening – one after another – of Wynn's Mirage (1989) and Bennett's Excalibur (1990) was the turning point that initiated what we could call a real race to design and build resorts ever more magnificent and ambitious, that would last for the entire decade of the 1990s. Considering that, absent any unforeseen events, between the first idea and the inauguration of a resort four to five years time are needed – for designing, financing and construction – we see immediately that the rebirth of Sin City has its roots in the years of sustained economic growth that started in the second half of 1982, during the first Reagan Administration, and that came to an end in 1989.

Let's now try to complete the story so far, listing all the casino hotels built along the Strip in those years, remembering that – before the Mirage – no major resort had been raised in Vegas since the Caesars

Palace (1966), apart from the Harrah's, born as Holiday Casino in 1973. It will become immediately apparent how the boom of the 1990s radically changed the city's face.

MIRAGE, November 22, 1989 (see chapter 16)

The resort that kicked off the Las Vegas revival. The first, genuine super-casino to open its doors. A mega-resort of 3,000 rooms (the Caesars Palace, though immense and spectacular, had "only" 1,300 rooms at the time) and with a casino of almost 100,000 square feet. The first one whose construction was funded directly by Wall Street, through the junk bonds fashionable at the time. A milestone.

RIO, January 15, 1990

The first resort to experiment the concept of standard rooms larger than usual (starting at 500 sq. ft.), well ahead of the Venetian, hence its full name: Rio All-Suite Hotel & Casino. It's not exactly on the Strip, but it can be considered part of this area of town. Inaugurated with only 430 rooms, over the years it got to over 2,500, thanks to the 52-story Masquerade Tower, completed in 1997 (the original tower is called Ipanema Tower). The Brazilian inspiration is evident both in the name and in the style of the interiors, and in the revealing attire of the cocktail waitresses too. The casino has an area of 117,000 sq. ft. Rio's importance to all poker players and fans is obvious, since it hosts – from the 2005 edition – the WSOP tournaments, the world poker championship in all its variants, attracting thousands of participants between June and July of each year. Also famous is the nightclub on the 51st floor of the Masquerade Tower, called Voodoo Lounge.

EXCALIBUR, June 19, 1990 (see chapter 18).

CASINO ROYALE, January 1, 1992 (not a property worth dwelling on).

LUXOR, October 15, 1993 (see chapter 19).

TREASURE ISLAND, October 27, 1993 (see chapter 20).

MGM GRAND, December 18, 1993 (see chapter 21).
On New Year's Day 1994, Frank Sinatra performed here for the last time in Las Vegas, 43 years after his first performance in Desert Inn's showroom.

HARD ROCK, March 10, 1995
Here is another resort that is not located right on the Strip, but that's worth mentioning anyway. For Las Vegas standards, both the hotel (650 rooms) and the casino (30,000 square feet) are small. The main feature of this resort, which allows it to survive among the giants, is that it is almost exclusively geared toward

a much younger clientele than the average Vegas casino hotel, a crowd largely coming from California – it certainly does not attract many locals –, mostly well endowed. A "young, hip crowd", as they say. It is no coincidence that the two most important keys to this resort's success are The Joint, the 4,000-seat showroom where some of the world's most famous musicians and bands have performed (such as: Rolling Stones, Guns N 'Roses, David Bowie, Cold Play, Oasis, Alicia Keys, Paul McCartney and many more), and Rehab, the forerunner of all day pool parties – nowadays to be found almost everywhere –, where every Sunday the most tireless visitors to Sin City sober up from the Saturday night hangover... with a new binge in the sun, around and in the pool! The two unavoidable ingredients of any pool party are alcohol and silicone, in varying proportions. Some people just seem to be insatiable...

STRATOSPHERE TOWER, April 30, 1996

When it opened, the Stratosphere replaced the Vegas World of Bob Stupak, at the northern end of the Strip. This resort owes its reputation only to the ultrahigh observation tower, the tallest in the United States at 1,149 feet (but ranked only 17th in the world). Located far from the center of the action, in a stretch of the Strip which is hardly reachable on foot and potentially unsafe at night, this casino hotel has always been getting by on the verge of bankruptcy and is currently owned by a subsidiary of Goldman Sachs. Contrary to a well-established tradition, it seems that the restaurant on top of the tower offers a commendable cuisine, with the added bonus – as you would expect – of a breathtaking view.

MONTE CARLO, June 21, 1996

Perhaps the most useless of all Strip resorts. In theory, it should recall the small but very affluent town of the same name on the Côte d'Azur, France, but the theme is definitely too bland – just think of more convincing characterization examples, such as the New York New York right next door, the Venetian, Paris Las Vegas – and the name would make sense only if it was a luxury casino hotel, in the mold of the Wynn Las Vegas to name one, which it is not. Instead, it is not exactly luxury that prevails throughout the resort, but rather mediocrity. Born as a 50% joint venture between Steve Wynn's Mirage Resorts and Circus Circus Enterprises, it was originally destined to be called Victoria. The name was changed at the last minute, but the blandness of the entire project remained. My impression is that they simply wanted to take advantage of the boom that was emerging in those years: the plot of land was available and it would have been a shame to leave it empty to dry in the sun. The cost of the resort, amounting to just $ 344 million ($ 540 million 2017) for 3,000 rooms, at a time of resorts costing billions gives the idea of the type of concept behind this property.

On November 26, 1996, Las Vegas loses the Sands (see chapters 5 and 9 for its glorious history), imploded by Sheldon Adelson to make way for his Venetian. Right in the midst of Vegas's second youth, this date marks the definitive closure of the romantic (and fictionalized) era of the city.

NEW YORK NEW YORK, January 3, 1997

The name says it all. Its 2,000 rooms are distributed in various buildings that replicate the exterior appearance of some of New York City's best known skyscrapers. So much so that it is perhaps the only hotel on the Strip where the endless corridors on the room floors can be interrupted abruptly, to continue after passing a sort of "chicane". There is also a copy of the Statue of Liberty at scale 1 to 2, a mini-Brooklyn Bridge and the famous Coney Island-inspired roller coaster. Also in this case, we are far from the investment required for modern Strip giants: this casino hotel did cost $ 460 million at the time (just over $ 700 million 2017).

BELLAGIO, October 15, 1998

We have repeatedly mentioned this impressive resort throughout the narration. We can add that this was the new leap forward in quality of Steve Wynn, after building the Mirage and the Treasure Island.

Confirming a sort of fixation of Wynn's for the French language, which we shall encounter again later on, the project was launched under the name of Beau Rivage, later dismissed as too generic. As already mentioned, the Bellagio definitively closes the era of the Strip for families, introducing – and for Las Vegas this is an absolute novelty – the era of great chefs and starred restaurants. Today the Strip is one of the world's culinary capitals (just check the restaurant guides for confirmation), but only 15 years ago this would have been unimaginable. In this resort, for example, you can dine at the Picasso restaurant, surrounded by original works by the painter Pablo Picasso.

The source of inspiration for the project is obvious: Lake Como in Italy and the village of Bellagio, that gave the name to the resort and the idea for the artificial lake that has become – with its extraordinary fountains dancing at the rhythm of music – the main free tourist attraction of the city. The architectural style and the interiors are, therefore, Italian, and are certainly more discreet and less flashy than those over at the Venetian. Among the focal points of the resort are the incredible multicolored glass sculpture by artist Dale Chihuly that overlooks the hotel lobby – every piece has been blown by specialized artisans in Venice, Italy –, the small but charming and well-kept botanical garden whose appearance radically changes with the seasons, and the art gallery, which hosts a series of ever-new exhibitions. It was, at the time, the most expensive resort ever built, with a $ 1.6 billion price tag (about $ 2.4 billion 2017) for 3,000 rooms and a 156,000 sq. ft. casino.

A cinematographic curiosity: the *Ocean's 11* remake of 2001 was set in part at the Bellagio and the scene of a stunning Julia Roberts descending a staircase to head towards the lobby of the hotel owned by her lover – played by Andy Garcia – was shot at this resort. The staircase in question, however, no longer exists, having been removed during the construction of the additional hotel tower (the smaller one, on the left of the main building), called the Spa Tower and inaugurated on December 23, 2004, with a thousand rooms. Precisely Andy Garcia turns out to be a decent pianist and, during the pauses of the filming, from time to time he loved to perform at the piano of a hotel lounge. A little reminiscence of the times of the first *Ocean's 11* and the unforgettable Rat Pack!

MANDALAY BAY, March 2, 1999

Here we find a very good example of a theme that's been implemented with some grace, discernible but not overwhelming, which has contributed to the remarkable success always enjoyed by this resort, despite its decentralized position quite far away from the Strip's heart. This is the first resort one sees coming from California and represents the attempt made by Circus Circus Enterprises – under the guidance of its two new top men, Clyde Turner and

Glenn Schaeffer – to get rid of the low to mid-range operator image (Circus Circus, Excalibur, Luxor) and target a more demanding and younger clientele. The project's final cost amounted to $ 950 million ($ 1.4 billion today), for the construction of a tower of forty golden glass-covered floors that is rather spectacular.

Of the 3,700 total rooms, 400 – located on the last five floors of the hotel – are managed by the renowned Four Seasons chain. The inspiring theme of the resort is vaguely tropical and its name was taken from the ancient capital of the Burmese empire (until the arrival of the British in 1885): Mandalay. The spectacular main pool, capable of generating waves crashing on a sandy beach (2,700 tons arduously carried on site), is home to numerous outdoor concerts during the summer months. Chef Alain Ducasse's Rivea restaurant, located on top of the Delano – a second tower of a thousand suites, inaugurated in 2003 as THEhotel –, is considered one of the very best in the city and features some tables set outdoors, directly overlooking the Strip. As you can imagine, the view is breathtaking.

VENETIAN, May 3, 1999 (see previous chapter).

PARIS LAS VEGAS, September 1, 1999

Definitely one of the most easily recognizable resorts of the entire Strip, thanks to its perfect reproduction of the Eiffel Tower at scale 1 to 2 (540 feet high). It seems that the original project called for the Eiffel Tower to be rebuilt in full size but that the idea was abandoned for security reasons. The façade replicates those of the Opéra Garnier and the Louvre, while right next to it there's the Arc de Triomphe, at scale 2 to 3. The resort, costing about $ 800 million (just shy of $ 1.2 billion 2017), houses two very distinctive restaurants, the Eiffel Tower Restaurant, from where you can enjoy spectacular views of Bellagio's dancing fountains and chosen – needless to say – for countless birthdays, anniversaries and wedding proposals, and Mon Ami Gabi, one of the rare examples in Vegas of a restaurant with outdoor seating right on the Strip sidewalk, almost like in Rome or Paris.

We need to highlight that over this decade Clark County's population – including both Downtown Las Vegas and the Strip – grew from 741,000 (1990) to 1,375,000 (2000) residents, virtually doubling. This is the time when telephone companies were forced to print two phone books every year to keep up with the population growth. As a consequence of such rapid growth, inevitably there are problems with water consumption – with the implementation of strict rules concerning, for instance, when and how to water all public and private green areas – and of other nature, such as a shortage of school buildings and hospitals. Meanwhile, however, the county population has stabilized around two million residents (see Appendix A).

24

THE NEW MILLENNIUM

Riding the wave of enthusiasm following a decade of truly extraordinary growth and the apparently unstoppable increase of real estate prices, partly fueled – as we would understand a few years later – by the irresponsible behavior of greedy and unscrupulous bankers, the early years of the new millennium were characterized by even grander projects. Some of them would never see the light of day, once the huge real estate bubble that was artificially created exploded. Let's briefly list the major resorts planned and built in the period 2000-2010, as well as those miserably failed long before they could open to the public.

PLANET HOLLYWOOD (ex ALADDIN), August 18, 2000

The exceedingly troubled story of this resort deserves a brief insight. The plot where it is located had been the site of a casino hotel since the 1960s, when Milton Prell bought a hotel named Tally Ho, which was in financial trouble after not being able to obtain a casino license. After some renovations, Prell reopened the resort with the new name of Aladdin on April 1, 1966. At that time, it hosted the largest casino on the entire Strip. It was here that Elvis Presley married his Priscilla on May 1, 1967. Some years later, a second 19-story tower was added (1972), but the resort never became profitable, changing ownership several times before being closed once and for all in 1997, to be imploded the following year.

The new Aladdin opened at eight o'clock in the morning of August 18, 2000, after the official inauguration scheduled for the previous evening had been delayed by county inspectors due to problems with the fire system. As a result of the unexpected delay, many customers found themselves out of baggage – already dropped off at the hotel – and a bed for the night. We can say that this big resort of over 2,500 rooms, costing $ 1.4 billion (about $ 2 billion 2017), was not born under a lucky star. Nor would it ever get the fame and success that many of its predecessors along the Strip had enjoyed.

Long story short, the Aladdin would always find itself in dire straits, financially speaking, filing for Chapter 11 bankruptcy already in September 2001. A partnership formed by Planet Hollywood and Starwood Hotels, one of the premier high-end hotel chains, took over the property in June 2003 and started a series of modernization works without closing it to the public. On April 17, 2007, the resort was again "inaugurated", this time under the sign of Planet Hollywood. Today, this casino hotel is part of Caesars Entertainment Corporation, one of the two casino industry giants that form the virtual duopoly dominating the entire length of the Strip.

WYNN LAS VEGAS, April 28, 2005

After being ousted from the company he had built and made great, Mr. Wynn decided he would just build a second one, possibly even more successful than his first. To understand how high Wynn was aiming this time, it is enough to consider the final cost of this resort, built on the ashes of the Desert Inn, partly imploded in 2001 and partly in 2004: $ 2.7 billion (equivalent to $ 3.4 billion today). Being a hotel of 2,700 rooms, we are talking about an average construction cost (for the whole resort) of 1 million per room, unprecedented in the hotel industry. Clearly, such figures would be unthinkable in the absence of a constant flow of revenue that goes well beyond the simple room rate, which comes from the casino, from the evening shows, night clubs and luxury restaurants, as well as from the many shops in the commercial area of the resort.

Continuing to flirt with the French language, Wynn had initially wanted to give the resort the name Le Rêve (the dream, in French), but he was persuaded to make use of his own name, for the first time, because it had become so iconic in Las Vegas to be immediately recognizable to the vast majority of visitors. Thus was born the idea for a wonderful commercial – to be found on YouTube – in which Wynn, from the top of the new Strip behemoth, looking straight into the camera said: «I'm Steve Wynn and this is my new hotel, the only one I've ever signed my name to.» Cool!

Le Rêve, however, remained: it's the name of the resident show, created at the time by Franco Dragone, one of the minds behind the success of Cirque du Soleil. The show, as you would expect, is colossal, and takes place largely in an aquatic setting, so much so that all 90 performers are certified scuba divers. As a testament to its extraordinary quality, Le Rêve has been voted "best production show" in Vegas for seven consecutive years by the 400 concierges working in the city.

A major change introduced by Wynn with this resort concerns the free shows open to anyone walking on the Strip sidewalk that Wynn had made the trademark of his previous projects. While the Mirage, Treasure Island and Bellagio did owe part of their fame to the rather elaborate productions that attracted non-paying onlookers outside of the resorts (the erupting volcano of the Mirage, the pirate battle of the Treasure Island and the dancing fountains of the Bellagio), with the property that bore his name Wynn decided to go in a different direction: beautiful gardens, elaborate fountains and spectacular waterfalls were reserved for the eyes of the resort guests, or at least for its visitors. Wynn even built a small artificial hill to hide from passersby the sight of the treats situated within the confines of the resort. Unquestionably, a proper U-turn by this volcanic entrepreneur.

It must be said that, from a purely architectural point of view, this time the building conceived by Wynn was not particularly original: a slightly curved tower of about fifty floors covered in bronzed glass. Quite similar to an elegant office skyscraper in Houston or Los Angeles, if you will. The same, identical style would be used by Wynn for the casino hotel that he would build a few years later.

ENCORE LAS VEGAS, December 22, 2008

Combining his never satiated love for the French language and a good degree of self-irony, this is how Wynn decided to name his second project of his second life as a visionary builder of the Strip. Once again, a spectacular commercial was produced that saw Wynn, seated at the very top of his new hotel tower, 192 meters above ground, close as follows: «Next time, we do this in the lobby.» Brilliant!

The rooms at the Encore are probably Vegas's most spacious (at 745 sq. ft.) and most elegantly appointed standard rooms, as confirmed by numerous hotel guides. Costing $ 2.3 billion total for slightly more than 2,000 rooms, it is quite obvious that Wynn did spare no expense. The Wynn-Encore complex hosts some of the finest restaurants in town and the only golf club located on the Strip north of the Mandalay Bay.

It has to be said: Steve Wynn might be losing his

eyesight, due to a condition called *retinitis pigmentosa* (RP), but he certainly hasn't lost his touch.

CITY CENTER, December 2009

The complex called City Center is the most ambitious project ever developed on the Las Vegas Strip and the largest private construction project in US history. It is basically an entire district of 76 acres, with hotels (the Aria, which hosts a casino of 150,000 sq. ft., and the Mandarin Oriental), obviously a large number of restaurants, a shopping center dedicated almost exclusively to luxury brands (Crystals), a condo-hotel (the Vdara) and a two-tower condominium with a particularly original architecture (the Veer Towers). An elevated tram connects the complex to the Bellagio to the north and the Monte Carlo to the south.

It was MGM Mirage, the company born from the takeover of Steve Wynn's Mirage Resorts by Kirk Kerkorian's MGM Grand Inc., to design this project, for a total investment of over $ 9 billion. Conceived during the real estate euphoria of the 2000s, the complex had the misfortune of being built during the severe economic recession following the bursting of the real estate bubble in 2007-2008 and opened its doors at the end of it, so that MGM Mirage – burdened by a $ 13 billion debt load at the time –, in order to guarantee the necessary financing to complete the work, had to sell a 50% stake to the investment firm Dubai World, the financial arm of the Dubai government. 2009 was

144

also the darkest year of the recent Las Vegas past, with the lowest number of visitors since 2003. Already in 2010, however, the recovery would begin, and in 2016 the overall record of visitors to the city would be updated, with 42,936,000 total guests (+ 18% compared to 2009).

In the City Center area there was also an example of resounding failure: what was supposed to be the Harmon Hotel, a casino-free hotel with an original elliptical shape, revealed a series of construction defects that forced the owners to dismantle it piece by piece between 2014 and 2015 without it ever operating. The financial loss caused by this fiasco is estimated at $ 400 million.

COSMOPOLITAN, December 15, 2010

This casino hotel, simply known as The Cosmo, did have a troubled origin indeed and it seriously risked suffering the same fate as the Fontainebleau farther north along the Strip, which never opened.

In fact, the original developer, Bruce Eichner, had to default on a $ 768 million loan in 2008, leaving the property on the books of Deutsche Bank, one of Europe's leading banking groups. They tried to sell it for years, finally reaching an agreement with private equity and asset management firm Blackstone Group only in May 2014 and collecting $ 1.73 billion. Having cost a grand total of $ 3.9 billion to design and build, in the end this project caused a $ 2.2 billion loss to

Deutsche Bank, to be added to all the other billions already lost in the wake of the Great Recession.

In spite of all the setbacks, The Cosmopolitan is a beautiful resort and a very successful one. Its hotel accommodations are considered among the best in town, its lobby is quite spectacular, in a "techno-cool" sort of way, and its all-you-can-eat buffet (Wicked Spoon) is generally considered a clever choice.

BIG FAILURES

The Great Recession has left three very visible scars on the Las Vegas Strip. The Fontainebleau Resort project was announced in May 2005 and was intended to be a sister property to the Fontainebleau Miami Beach, the very hotel where Steve Wynn had met his wife-to-be, Elaine Pascal. But the project was never properly funded and, despite having Glenn Schaeffer at the helm – former president of Mandalay Resort Group and one of the most experienced men in the business –, by 2009 it was in shambles. In November of that year, investor Carl Icahn bought the property in bankruptcy court for just $ 156 million total. The previous owners had already sank almost $ 2 billion in it. After auctioning off the furnishing previously intended for the building, Icahn sold it again to investment firms Witkoff Group and New Valley LLC in August 2017. By some estimates, it would now cost about $ 1.2 billion to $ 1.5 billion to complete the project and to open a functioning resort comprising a

95,000 sq. ft. casino, about 3,000 hotel rooms and maybe 1,000 condominiums. Vegas locals and all visitors are left with an utterly anonymous 68-story blue monolith located two blocks north of the Encore.

A similar fate has befallen two other gigantic projects in those years. One was called the Echelon Place and was announced in January 2006 by Boyd Gaming Corp., a gaming and hospitality company with interests also in Las Vegas. It was meant to replace the Stardust and Westward Ho casino hotels, just south of the Circus Circus, and had a projected cost of $ 4 billion. A series of different buildings was planned, including hotel towers, a convention center and a shopping center. Nothing of the sort happened. In March 2013, Boyd Gaming decided to sell the Echelon site to a Malaysia-based casino company, the Genting Group, for $ 350 million. Considering the expenses incurred for the land and a very partial construction of the resort, this ill fated adventure meant a loss of roughly $ 1 billion for Boyd.

The other one never even started construction and the big lot where it was supposed to rise lies idle to this day. We are talking about a project called Las Vegas Plaza, launched by the El-Ad Group, an Israel-based real estate development company. When announced, in December 2007, it was planned to include no less than seven different buildings, for a total of 4,100 hotel rooms and 2,600 condominium units. It would host the largest casino on the Strip (175,000 sq. ft.) and would have a not too shabby price tag of at least $ 5 billion. In the end, the only one happy with the entire endeavor was Mr. Phil Ruffin (who would later become the owner of the Treasure Island), who was smart enough to sell the land formerly occupied by the New Frontier to El-Ad in May 2007, at the very peak of the housing bubble. In fact, this deal marked a new Strip record of $ 33 million per acre, allowing Ruffin to collect a cool $ 1.2 billion for the property. Suffice it to say that none of the imposing towers designed for the site ever saw a single construction worker.

25

WHAT FUTURE?

The greatest threat today to the survival of Las Vegas as a gambling, convention and tourist Mecca isn't shortage of visitors but shortage of water. Sitting in an especially arid area with very little annual precipitation, the town has always been closely dependent on the reservoir of Lake Mead, created by the construction of the Hoover Dam on the Colorado River, about 24 miles from the Strip. Originally and for many years the largest reservoir in the States, for the last four years it has actually been smaller than the second largest US reservoir, Lake Powell at the border between Utah and Arizona. Due to a combination of recurring droughts and ever increasing water demands from three states (Nevada, Arizona and California), since 1983 Lake Mead has never reached full capacity and today holds less than half the water it should. Those are scary numbers, if you ask me.

On the financial side, the more savvy gaming corporations have secured their future by expanding operations to Macao, the new frontier of the global casino business. The territory of Macao, a former Portuguese colony returned under Chinese jurisdiction at the end of 1999, is directly connected to China, with its population of 1.4 billion people, including many with a high propensity to gambling. Similarly to Hong Kong, at least on paper Macao enjoys some degree of autonomy from the Chinese central government for about fifty years.

Just as Las Vegas's, Macao's economy depends largely on tourism and casinos. Traditionally, since 1962 – thanks to a government concession – the entire casino industry had been a monopoly in the hands of a company of tycoon Stanley Ho, originally from Hong Kong. Things changed radically in 2002, when the exclusive concession did expire and the Macao government decided to open its gambling market to other operators, including foreign ones, and announced an invitation to tender for gaming licenses. Over the years, six casino operator concessions were awarded, including three to American companies active in Las Vegas: Wynn Resorts led by Steve Wynn, Las Vegas Sands led by Sheldon Adelson and MGM Resorts International. Basically, the only major Strip player to remain excluded from the booming Chinese market is Caesars Entertainment Corp., which is however the largest US operator nationwide. As for the other three protagonists of the Strip, today they draw a large share of their profits from casinos opened on the faraway Macao peninsula, where – for various reasons – owning casinos is on average much more profitable than in the US.

Back in Vegas, the only major project in the works

along the Strip is the new resort announced by Genting Group, by the name of Resorts World and with a decidedly Asian theme, right where Boyd's Echelon Place was expected to rise. With an estimated price tag of $ 7.2 billion and some 6,500 rooms distributed over four hotel towers, it's no small task for sure. In fact, the construction timetable has been pushed forward several times and the resort is now scheduled to be inaugurated in 2020. We'll see.

APPENDIX A
CLARK COUNTY POPULATION
(includes the Las Vegas area)

1910	3,321
1920	4,859
1930	8,532
1940	16,414
1950	48,289
1960	127,016
1970	273,288
1980	463,087
1990	741,459
2000	1,375,765
2010	1,951,269
2016 est.	2,155,664

APPENDIX B
MAJOR STRIP CASINO COMPANIES

<u>Caesars Entertainment Corp.</u> (47 properties globally in 5 countries)
- Caesars Palace (including the Nobu Hotel)
- Harrah's
- Bally's
- Flamingo
- Paris
- Planet Hollywood
- Rio
- The Cromwell (formerly Barbary Coast)
- The Linq (formerly Imperial Palace)

<u>MGM Resorts International</u> (27 properties globally in the US, Macao and China)
- MGM Grand
- Bellagio
- Aria
- Vdara
- Mandalay Bay (including the Delano)
- Mirage
- Monte Carlo
- New York-New York
- Luxor
- Excalibur
- Circus Circus

<u>Las Vegas Sands Corp.</u> (9 properties in the US, Singapore and Macao)
- The Venetian
- The Palazzo

<u>Wynn Resorts Ltd.</u> (5 properties in Las Vegas and Macao)
- Wynn Las Vegas
- Encore at Wynn Las Vegas